KU-657-124

Wicca
for everyday living

Wicca
for everyday living

The definitive guide to magic and the craft

Ann-Marie Gallagher

Bounty
BOOKS

Publisher: Samantha Warrington
Editorial & Design Manager: Emma Hill
Production Controller: Sarah Kramer
Packaged by Guy Croton Publishing Services,
Tonbridge, Kent

This edition reprinted in 2016, 2017

First published in 2014 by Bounty Books,
a division of Octopus Publishing Group Ltd
Carmelite House
50 Victoria Embankment
London EC4Y 0DZ
www.octopusbooks.co.uk

An Hachette UK Company
www.hachette.co.uk

Reprinted in 2015

Material previously published in *The Wicca Bible*
(Gaia, 2005)

Copyright © 2014 Octopus Publishing Group Ltd
Photography © Octopus Publishing Group Ltd
Text copyright Ann-Marie Gallagher 2005

All rights reserved. No part of this work may be
reproduced or utilized in any form
or by any means, electronic or mechanical, including
photocopying, recording or by any
information storage and retrieval system, without the
prior written permission of the publisher.

ISBN: 978-0-753728-51-2

A CIP catalogue record for this book is available from the
British Library

Printed and bound in China

CONTENTS

INTRODUCTION

Wicca is the religion and practice of witches, or 'the Wise', as we are sometimes known. It has been described as the fastest-growing religion in the West, though nobody really knows how many Wiccans there are in the world. Judging by the number of internet sites and formal groups cropping up around the globe, particularly in Britain, continental Europe and the USA, it is clear that the growth of the Wiccan movement is quite phenomenal. Perhaps this is not all that surprising.

AT ONE WITH NATURE

Over the last few decades, public interest in the environment, in alternative healing therapies, self-development, holistic food and medicine, social justice and, significantly, in 'alternative' spiritualities and magic has developed tremendously. Wicca explores many of these concerns within an inclusive spiritual path that honours the diversity and divinity of nature and advises its followers to 'harm none'. If you read carefully through the different sections of this book, participate in the activities it guides you through and learn more about practising Wicca, you will begin to understand exactly why Wicca, sometimes called 'the Craft', has grown in popularity and why, in the twenty-first century, more and more people are declaring themselves 'Wicce' or 'Witches'.

Because Wicca is a religion that does not have a doctrine or a set central priesthood, sacred texts or sets of rules, the responsibility for learning and growing within the chosen spiritual path is placed upon the individual. Even though there are some established traditions within the Wiccan community, many have grown out of exploration and continue to evolve as Wiccans learn which practices and points of understanding are essential, and which are more flexible.

Practising spirituality outside the limiting strictures of a set 'organized' religion can be a very liberating experience, but it can also be extraordinarily demanding on the individual, requiring considerable resourcefulness. Some novices will be lucky enough to have friends or family who are Wiccan, and thus have good sources of advice only

Wicca is a nature religion. Wiccans see the divine in nature, both within us and around us.

The chalice is a symbol of healing, communion and initiation.

a phone call away. The majority of us, though, start out with an interest that we want to explore privately before joining a group or sounding out others for counsel.

WICCA FOR ALL

The main purpose of this book is to provide a resource of information – and inspiration – both for those who are encountering Wicca for the first time and for those who are already treading that path. It discusses the key aspects of Wicca and will help direct you through the exciting territory that is Wiccan spirituality

and practice, and help you develop your own understanding and sense of the spiritual on your travels.

Welcome, then, to Wicca as it is practised by the Wise, with its regional variations and in its diverse flavours all over the globe. Welcome also to a tradition that casts a look over its shoulder into the past to find a spiritual affinity with our ancestors, and looks forward to the future for new ways of living with each other, with the rhythms of the Earth and nature. And if you are about to set your foot on the path of the Wise for the first time, then as the Wicce say, Blessed Be.

Wicca works with the rhythms and tides of nature.

HOW TO USE THE BOOK

For the beginner, the best and most effective way to use this book when reading it for the first time is to work through it in order, trying the various exercises as you proceed. It is also best, if you are new to Wicca, to read through What is Wicca? (see pages 12–41), which will give you a good foundation for what follows. Each section has an introductory segment with background and guidance to the information and exercises that follow.

It is important to read the introductions carefully as they often define and explain terminology and provide information vital to the practical work in the sections. For example, the introduction to Visualization (see pages 84–89) offers a beginner's guide to visualization, including practical guidance on how to prepare physically and how to create the sacred space in which to work. Ignoring this advice may adversely affect your progress through the exercises and lead to frustration. In particular, if you are tempted to dip into the spells in Spell-work and Rituals (see pages 144–173), it is vital that you read the introduction explaining principles, laws and ethics..

Good resource material can be found in the Eight Sabbats (see pages 42–65) as well as some suggested activities for attuning to the five sacred Elements (see pages 66–81).

Preparation is important. This witch censes the space prior to ritual.

Traditionally, handfasting lasts for a year and a day.

In The Sacred Circle (see pages 114–143) you will find guidance on the timing of spells and rituals, including moon and sun cycles, days of the week, planetary hours and astrological information. In addition, there is a wealth of practical advice and information on the everyday business of Wicca, including how to put together an altar, acquire and consecrate magical tools and cast a circle (sacred space).

PRACTISING WICCANS

For the more experienced, it is still a good idea to read through What is Wicca? Beyond that, your own personal experience will enable you to dip in and out of the book at will for information, ideas and inspiration for your work. This book should help you build and enhance your knowledge and skills in the Craft. Bright blessings on the path!

WHAT IS WICCA?

WICCA – WHAT IT IS AND WHAT IT IS NOT

These days, Wicca refers to a set of practices, beliefs and traditions associated with people who call themselves witches. Witches call themselves Wicca ('wise' in Anglo-Saxon), not because they think they know more or better than anyone else, but because, historically, this expression referred to people who worked with nature and magic. In Wicca, wisdom is an aspiration rather than a starting point, and learning is an ongoing process.

Wiccans use a broomstick to prepare sacred spaces.

This requires those who wish to join the ranks of 'the Wise' to acknowledge and accept the constant processes of change and development both within us and within the world around us. This adaptability would seem to be appropriate as, apparently, a secondary meaning of the word 'Wicca' was 'bendy' or 'wiggly'!

On the subject of meaning, there is a distinction between the way that the word 'Wicca' tends to be interpreted in Britain and its customary usage in North America.

References to 'Wicca' in Britain have traditionally alluded to a specific initiatory system of witchcraft as practised within covens that follow either Alexandrian or Gardnerian witchcraft, or a synthesis of both sometimes called British or English traditional witchcraft. This definition of the term excludes solo

Ancient pagan temple, Delphi, Greece.

practitioners of the craft, and those groups who are rather more eclectic in their practices.

In North America, the term is used in a more inclusive way – it refers to all those who number themselves among 'the Wise', whether solo practitioners or members of groups who fall outside the Alexandrian/ Gardnerian definition. In this book, I take this latter sense in which the term is applied – and I am happy to report that references to Wicca in Britain are shifting slowly towards this more all-embracing definition.

MODERN WICCA

Founded by Gerald Gardner, Gardnerian witchcraft forms the basis of modern wicca. Embracing ancient traditions, it uses the pattern of the ritual circle and elemental quarters for Air, Fire, Earth and Water. Alexandrian wicca is a development of Gardnerian wicca, and incorporates elements of Judaeo-Christian sources, as well as aspects of the Greek and Egyptian mysteries and Celtic traditions. It also uses the now widely recognized colour symbolism set out on pages 30–33.

WHAT THEN, IS WICCA?

It is both a spiritual tradition (which is why it is a religion) and a set of practices (which is why it is sometimes called 'the Craft'). Some Wiccans honour a God and Goddess, while others honour a Goddess in whom the two roles are united. We work with the seasons and tides of the Earth, and the rhythms of the Moon, planets and stars. Wiccans see the divine in nature, both within and around us, as we are considered part of nature rather than standing outside of it. In this sense, we see the divine as immanent (meaning 'residing within') within nature, and within ourselves. We also have a sense of the spirit of all things that exist, including rocks, trees, animals and places, as well as people. This is why we sometimes refer to them as 'beings' – it is because we honour their individual as well as their integral, or 'connected', existence. Wiccans place great emphasis on 'connection' as we see all matter and all beings as interrelated and interdependent. The symbol for this sense of interconnection is the web – a network of existence through which all beings are linked.

This concept of relatedness is present in all of our rituals and practices, whether spells for healing, rites for marking the seasons, or changes in our lives. If we are part of that wider, connected web, then everything we do affects all things within it. The magical spells we perform key in a particular pattern to be sent further along the web to effect change. Our rituals are signals that something is happening in our lives, and the full realization of this is felt in our communities and in our everyday experiences. It also affects our everyday actions and colours our approach to ethics and behaviour. What we do counts: shake one part of the web and the whole structure trembles, so we need to be sure that our actions do not harm. An injury to one, is an injury to all. A central tenet that unites all Wiccans is attendance to what is known as 'the Wiccan Rede', which says: 'An it harm none, do thy will' (if it harms none, go ahead). As a moral aspiration, it is a worthy one, and Wicca is a religion that takes a responsible approach to its relationship with all beings.

A SPIRITUAL PATH

Wicca places great responsibility on its followers to acknowledge and appreciate divinity within all nature, to place love and respect at the forefront of our relationships, and to ensure that harm is caused to none. What it is not is the stereotype of the Devil-worshipper setting curses to do harm or to gain power over others. Devils are not part of our theology and we go out of our way to avoid harming: neither make sense in the joyful, celebratory and responsible spiritual path that is Wicca.

Wicca is a path that emphasizes personal responsibility.

THE WICCAN REDE

'Rede', is a Middle English word, derived from Old English and Old High German, and it is thought to mean 'advice'. The Wiccan Rede is a guide to making decisions about how we act. The origins of the Rede are lost in the mists of time and the secrecy to which older working covens were bound, and there is some debate among Wiccan scholars about its historical roots. The Rede's broader meaning, however, is generally agreed; do what you will, but ensure that it harms no one.

HARM NONE

What Wiccans may differ on, is how far this tenet takes us in considering what 'harm' is, who count as the 'none' and how far we can practise this simple piece of guidance in a complex world.

Many Wiccans take their spiritual beliefs into the realm of political activism, particularly environmentalism, conservation, animal welfare and social justice. For some of us, if systems, organizations or corporations do harm, then we consider it part of our duty of care towards the Earth and other beings to get them to stop. This extends the interpretation of the Rede to incorporate a duty to prevent or stop harm. To paraphrase Edmund Burke: 'The only thing necessary for the triumph of evil is for good people to do nothing.' One interpretation of this is, therefore, that a lack of action can constitute harm.

However, what we cannot do – if we are to take the advice of the Wiccan Rede – is cause 'lesser' harms in order to prevent 'greater' harms. If we are to 'harm none', then 'harming none' means exactly what it says; the end cannot justify the means if the means are harmful. In short, the means are subject to the same rules as the ultimate goal of an action.

DO WHAT YE WILL

The first part of the Rede, 'harm none', is emphasized in Wiccan practice because of its ethical importance. The second part of the Rede is equally important. Its first public appearance, in 1971, was to a generation rebelling against authority and social conformity, and

The Rede is a guide and foundation to decision-making.

the advice to 'do what ye will' was particularly timely. However, the message to follow our own counsel is still relevant today; we live in an age where 'experts' constantly line up to tell us what to believe and how to live. What the Wiccan Rede does, is to remind us that we should have the confidence to trust our own good instincts and knowledge instead of succumbing to the contemporary tyranny of 'spin' over substance.

WICCAN SPIRITUALITY

Wicca is a nature religion. It sees the divine in all things, especially in the natural world, and takes the wonderful diversity that is in nature as its guide, celebrating divinity in all its manifestations. For Wiccans, nature is sacred because the divine is present within it, and because we are a part of nature, then we too are divine expressions of the God, Goddess or Great Spirit who connects all beings. The Mother Charge is a recitation by a priestess at esbats, the Full-Moon celebrations.

The Mother Charge encapsulates the importance to witches of the idea of the divine within nature and of nature as the divine. Because of this connection, there is a strong animistic tendency within the Wicca tradition, which sees Spirit in all things. Witches are also aware of *genii loci* or 'spirits of place', and when we are working magic or doing a circle outdoors, we make sure that we honour the local spirit of the place in which we choose to celebrate.

THE MOTHER CHARGE

The priestess speaks to
Her people and declares:

*I who am the beauty
of the green earth,*

*And the white moon
among the stars,*

And the mystery of the waters,

*Call unto your soul:
arise and come unto me,*

For I am the soul of nature...

HONOURING THE GODDESS

Wicca is a polytheistic religion – it does not adhere to one god or goddess, but honours the Goddess and God, sometimes Goddess alone in whom the two are united. We also honour various gods and goddesses (deities) – often seen as the Goddess in Her many aspects and names. There is a saying in Wicca that 'All gods and goddesses are one God or Goddess', to which is sometimes added the acknowledgement 'but

The web is a Wiccan symbol of Sprit and connection.

Wicca's gods and goddesses are honoured as friends and confidantes.

not all gods and goddesses are the SAME God or Goddess'. When we speak of 'the Goddess' or 'the God' we are talking of a being in whom all deities are united. When we speak of Demeter the Earth Goddess, Herne the Horned One, Lugh the Sun God, we see each one as aspects of 'the God or Goddess' and as individual deities in their own right.

Our relationships with our deities are generally close, even intimate. Because we see divinity as being immanent (within), we see our deities as being manifest within us and in the world around us. Since they do not stand apart from humanity or outside of nature and time, our deities are not interventionist – they do not call down judgement or demand sacrifices of us. On the contrary, they are our friends, confidantes, guides, parents, sisters and brothers, upon whom our thinking, feeling and instinctive selves call whenever we feel the need.

THE GODDESS WITHIN

If you have been used to thinking of the divine as separate from humanity and the everyday world, the idea that you can treat the God or Goddess as a friend might seem quite startling. But if the God or Goddess is a part of us, then we too are the God or Goddess. Talking to the divine in a familiar, friendly manner does not dishonour them; we are simply acknowledging and celebrating the life-affirming relationship we have with them. Of course, the relationship that one develops with the God or Goddess or particular deities is going to be unique and special. Just as we all deal with our personal relationships very differently, there is a variety of attitudes towards the deities within Wicca. But it is true to say that, for most of us, there is no contradiction in speaking to the God or Goddess as a friend, and lighting a candle to honour Him or Her.

Wiccan practice varies widely when it comes to the ways in which we conceptualize our deities. There is an approach that sees the God or Goddess as 'out there'; present in nature and manifest, for example, as a horned entity, or as a woman clothed in stars. There is another approach that sees the God or Goddess as wholly within nature and within ourselves. A third approach perceives the Deity as representational, as symbolic. For most witches, it is possible to believe all three at once – when I asked a witch friend whether the Deity was within the self, within nature or 'out there' as a distinctive entity, she smiled and replied 'yes'.

LIVING MAGICALLY

Wicca is a religion that combines two important elements: spirituality and magic. Although in most world religions the two are considered separate, in Wicca they are very closely intertwined. At one level, we see all acts of creation as inherently magical. For Wiccans, the most amazing magical event was the birth of the Universe. Smaller but no less wondrous examples of such magic take place around us all the time – but because we are so accustomed to them, we do not notice. Rediscovering this magic through learning and experience is part of the spiritual journey; hence the Wiccan interest in country lore, herbs, astronomy, and the rocks, stones and crystals that are the bones of the Earth. We study the ways of trees and the cycle of the seasons and the stars and planets in order to grow in knowledge. Our spirituality is pagan – like our pre-Christian ancestors we revere the spirit and magic of the natural world.

ACTS OF TRANSFORMATION

At another level, we acknowledge magic as a conscious act by which we seek both inward and outward transformation. Each magical act changes us in accordance with its nature. Because all things that exist are linked together and because we, too, are the God or Goddess, when we perform healing spells we send out healing to individuals who are also aspects of the whole, as well as effecting change within ourselves. This is linked to our notion of what

is 'spiritual' – how we understand our place within and relationship to all beings, the Earth, the Deity, the cosmos. When we call upon the elements, the spirit of nature, the Deity in our magical work, we are also celebrating our spirituality. For witches, magic is a spiritual act.

LOVE IS THE LAW

In Wicca, there is no moralistic doctrine or dogma other than the advice offered in the Wiccan Rede. We are constantly re-evaluating our understanding of what it means to be spirit-in-flesh. We see the body as co-extensive with the spirit, and consequently, as sacred. The Mother Charge tells us 'All acts of love and pleasure are my rituals'. The only 'law' here is love, and acts of love are performed in mutuality, with permission, and not to harm, control or disempower. In Wicca, physical pleasure is an act of worship. As spirit-in-flesh we honour and give value to the body through intense connection with another human being, and in turn connect with the God or Goddess through ecstasy. It matters not whether we are gay, straight, bisexual or transgendered – the physical world is sacred, and in celebrating our physicality, our sexuality and our human nature, we honour the Goddess, giver of all life, and soul of all nature.

The physical world is seen as co-extensive with Spirit, and therefore sacred.

WICCAN SYMBOLS

Wicca has its storehouse of favourite symbols. The attributes of some of them are multiple and subject to almost endless connotation and overlay. A number of very basic interpretations are generally agreed, however, and a brief glossary of these can be found on the pages that follow.

Witches often wear symbols and images on their clothing or in jewellery designs.

Occasionally, a symbol is carried or worn for a specific purpose, by way of invoking its power for protection or strength, for example. This is most often the case when we use symbols to decorate our magical tools, especially chalices, athames and wands or staffs. We also make good use of basic signatory symbols in magic and ritual by carving relevant signs into candles, writing them in ink or describing them in the air with our athames. Elemental and planetary symbols help to focus on the energies we invoke, and at the same time are encapsulations of their concentrated power.

THE PENTACLE/PENTAGRAM

One of the most commonly sported symbols in Wicca is the five-pointed star, the pentagram. If encircled it is a pentacle and signifies variously the circle of the Earth or the unified nature of the Universe. The five points pertain to the five sacred elements Air, Fire, Water, Earth and Spirit, and in this form it is worn with the point upwards. When a pentacle or pentagram is seen with the point downwards, this is a protective or banishing symbol and is sometimes found over doorways. The direction of the Elements symbolized by the five points varies, but a common one is shown in the diagram.

Spirit

Air

Fire

Earth

Water

SYMBOLS OF THE ELEMENTS

The colours for the five elements are Air–yellow, Fire–red, Water–blue, Earth–green, Spirit–purple or white. The symbol for each element is an equilateral triangle (see below).

AIR: point upwards, traversed by a horizontal line

FIRE: point upwards

SPIRIT: a pentagram, upwards pointing

EARTH: point downwards, traversed by a horizontal line

WATER: point downwards

THE SIX-POINTED STAR

In Wicca the six-pointed star unites the symbols of the four physical elements (see above) and its symmetry visibly demonstrates the Hermetic principle, 'As above, So below'. In Wicca, therefore, this is a symbol of Hermetic significance, as well as the conjunction of the four physical elements.

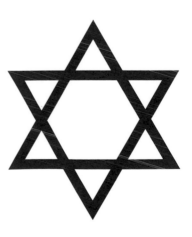

WEBS, MAZES, LABYRINTHS AND SPIRALS

The web is a particularly important symbol in contemporary Wicca; it describes the way in which we conceive of the physical and spiritual Universe and the nature of magic. It symbolizes sacred connection, which we also understand variously as Spirit and/or the God and Goddess.

Mazes are symbols of the left-brain functions. They represent rationality, logic and reason

Walking or tracing a labyrinth engages the right-brain functions, home of intuitive and psychic abilities. A labyrinth depicts the journey from birth, through life, to death and rebirth. This symbol is found on many of the ancient monuments of the world and is fundamental to a range of diverse world cultures.

The spiral has a similar function to the web, and denotes the microcosmic and macrocosmic order of the Universe. The spiral, like the web, is a symbol of the element of Spirit.

TRIANGLES, TRISKELES AND CELTIC KNOTS

Triplicity is a favourite configuration in Wicca and resonates with the mathematical and geometric philosophies of the ancient Greeks and with the spiritual symbols used by the Celts. Triskeles, the three-legged 'swirls' of Celtic art, depict the power of three – Earth, Water and Fire. Symbolically, they are similar to spirals, and because the number three is sacred to the Triple Moon Goddess, signify goddess energy.

THE EIGHT-SPOKED WHEEL

The eight-spoked wheel is a symbol of the sacred year, each spoke representing one of the seasonal Sabbats. It sometimes symbolizes the Wheel of Fortuna, goddess of chance and fate in the Roman pantheon.

THE ANKH AND THE EYE OF HORUS

The ankh is an ancient Egyptian symbol associated with Isis, the All-Mother and goddess of magic and healing. The loop is a yonic – female sexual – symbol, while the downward strut is phallic. In conjunction these bring forth life and so the ankh is seen as the key to fertility, rebirth and eternal life. The Eye of Horus, her divine son, is a protection against evil and a symbol of 'seeing' or wisdom. Horus is a god of health and regeneration, and so his symbol carries some significance for contemporary pagans.

THE GREEN MAN

Ancient depictions of the Green Man can be found all over the British Isles. In essence, he is a nature spirit, replete with leafy features and often with vegetation emerging from his mouth. In Wicca he is seen both as an aspect of the god and as a champion of environmentalism. The Green Man is associated with the festival of Beltane (see pages 58–59) and the coming of summer.

THE TRIPLE MOON

A Full Moon disc mounted on each side by waxing and waning crescents is a symbol of the Triple Moon goddess, Maiden, Mother and Crone respectively.

CORNUCOPIA

The Horn of Plenty is the symbol of the ancient Roman deity Ceres, goddess of fertility and abundance. The wearing of this symbol generally denotes a wish for abundance on the part of the bearer.

COLOURS

Some witches believe that different spiritual 'vibrations' are produced by different colours, a theory that moves beyond symbolism and is not peculiar to Wicca but more 'New Age' in origin. The glossary below restricts itself to the symbolic associations and correspondences of colour. The five sacred elements in Wicca have specific colours assigned to them (see page 70).

WHITE

The colour of the Moon, white is often used to invoke lunar energy in spell-work. It is also symbolic of purity and light and is often used in conjunction with other colours to denote these as aspects of the work we are undertaking. Blessing rituals generally use white candles. Because white promotes ideas of innocence, it can also be used to connote initiation and pure intentions.

Lunar energy is symbolized by silver or the colour white.

Red can be used to summon Martian energy.

BLACK

Contrary to popular belief, black is not a colour of 'evil' but the colour of potential, of space and protection. It is often used in banishment and binding spells as it is the colour denoting the dark part of the Moon as it wanes or the Dark Moon itself. Black symbolizes darkness; again, in Wicca not conceived of as 'evil' but as potentially creative and inward-reaching. This is a popular colour for candles if summoning the dark goddesses such as Hecate, Kali or the Morrigan.

RED

A primary colour denoting fire, passion, the will, courage and sexual energy, red is often used in love spells to summon true love. The colour of Martian energy, red is used in spell-work to summon defence against that which threatens or oppresses. Red is also denotes solar energy.

YELLOW

A primary colour denoting matters of the mind, communication, learning,

Blue is strongly connected with water associations.

movement and beginnings, yellow
is the colour of goddesses of intellect
and study such as the Greek goddess
Athene or the Hindu goddess
Sarasvarti, and of apprenticeship
and studenthood. As with red, yellow
can be used to invoke solar energy,
but it belongs chiefly to Mercury,
the planet of swift movement and
effective communication.

BLUE

This primary colour is used to
represent Water. Consequently is
stands for healing, harmony, love,
emotions, psychic abilities, dreams
and intuition. Blue is linked with
planet Neptune's energy, with the
darkest blues sometimes symbolizing
the planet Jupiter.

GREEN

A secondary colour symbolizing fertility, growth, material matters and the Earth, green is also linked with planet Venus's energy. Green is the colour of the heart chakra and symbolic of feelings, wholeness and harmonious conjunctions.

PURPLE

In ancient times regarded as the royal colour, purple is the colour of the planet Jupiter, once seen as king of the gods. Purple denotes spirituality, generosity, justice, serendipity and wonder. Purple is also the colour of transformation, which links it back to its association with the element of Spirit. A colour linked with Fortuna, goddess of the wheel of fate and chance and with Iris, the messenger goddess of the rainbow (see below).

PINK

This colour symbolizes affection, affinity, friendship; pink candles are sometimes used in love spells alongside red and white to add these particular qualities to the others required of a prospective lover.

SILVER

Like white, symbolic of lunar energy, silver is worn by many witches in

Green is a symbol of Earth energy.

preference to gold because of the emphasis on Moon phases and other lunar symbolism within Wicca. Silver can also symbolize the need for money in spells for wealth.

GOLD

Gold symbolizes the attributes of the Sun, including happiness, health, fulfilment, success and, according to alchemy, spiritual attainment. Gold is often used in spells to bring health to an individual or general success to an enterprise.

RAINBOW

Not one colour but multi-coloured, in Wicca the rainbow symbolizes hope, the close interconnection between sky and earth, spirituality and physicality, and the principles of connection, coalition and unity.

HERBAL LORE

Given the time-honoured association between witches and herbal knowledge, it is unsurprising that contemporary Wiccans draw on the traditions of magical herbalism. Just as there are symbolic correspondences between planets, constellations, Moon phases, days of the week, gods and goddesses and the elements, so there are traditions linking different plants to different magical or ritual purposes.

Many witches like to make their own herbal oils.

HERBAL SAFETY

It is important to note that the use of herbs in Wicca does not extend to medical prescriptions – medicinal herbalism is firmly based on medical research and study that takes many years and you should never 'prescribe' herbs to yourself or others to apply physically or take internally without the appropriate medicinal training. There is some interesting crossover between medicinal herbalism and magical herbalism, but in practice they need to be kept safely separate!

USING HERBS

Herbs can be used in a wide variety of ways within the Craft; as decoration for an altar, as part of an incense blend, in a 'balefire' – a fire set for magical or ritual purposes – or as stuffing in cloth poppets, 'fetishes' or manikins. Herbs can also be deployed in ritual or spell-work by anointing a candle with carrier oil and rolling it in the dried leaves and flowers before lighting it.

Another use of herbs in magic is to place them in pouches to be tied to a bedpost or worn as a pendant around the neck. Hanging bunches or wreaths of herbs with protective or banishing properties around a hearth in the central point of a household, or at the front and back doors, is an ancient way of protecting your home. Herbs can also be woven into chaplets to be placed around the base of ritual candles or into circlets to be worn on the heads of participants during circle work.

Some witches like to make their own herbed oil by steeping concentrated amounts of herb in a good oil, such as grapeseed, and leaving it for at least a week to absorb the scent and energy of the leaves. They then pour the oil from the jar or bottle onto a fresh set of leaves. This process should be repeated until the oil is thoroughly scented with the herbal perfume. Particularly successful herbs for this treatment are rosemary, basil, sage and thyme. This oil is considered extra-charged for magical use as the magician has already placed their energy into its preparation for sacred purposes. Both the energy and intent of the maker infuse the oil with a specfic type of energy that is helpful to spell-work.

FRESH IS BEST

Fresh herbs will always give out a different 'vibe' from that given out by dried herbs (which can still be used at a pinch), and it is handy to have the fresh variety on hand. Whenever you pick leaves and flowers from a plant, you should always ask for the plant's permission – silently or aloud. If the herbs come from your own garden, bury a crumb of bread soaked with wine at the base of the plant when you pick its leaves — as a special 'thank you' to the Earth.

Fresh and dried herbs have different energies.

OILS AND INCENSES

The use of scent in ritual can be a powerful aid to spiritual development and spell-work, with different perfumes promoting mood changes and altered states of consciousness. Both essential oils and incenses capture the essence of a plant and thus carry the concentrated energy of a plant's magical and spiritual properties. They can be used to good effect in circle- and meditation-work in a wide variety of ways.

Oils are particularly versatile. Only pure essential oils should be used for circle-work as these are natural essences encapsulating the plant qualities. Essential oils can be used in burners in the place of incense; they can also be used to anoint candles and help charge them with their energy, plus the energy of our intent and power-raising. Diluted essential oils can be used to anoint people for self-blessing – the level of concentration is particularly crucial here, however (see Caution on page 39).

If you are using an oil burner, note that the essential oil is usually added to water placed in the dish above a lit tea-light. If you intend using essential oil diluted with carrier oil such as grapeseed or almond, either for anointing a person or a candle, ensure that the dilute proportions are within safe limits. You will also need to keep a dry towel close at hand,

as oil spreads very quickly and can make hands and implements very slippery.

USING INCENSE

The use of incense in circles, particularly loose incense, can be dramatic and add to the atmosphere of the sacred space. It can be used with certain herbs to promote the altered states of consciousness that participants seek to achieve. Echoing the practices of our pagan ancestors, incense carries our wishes to the deities on the sweet, airborne smoke.

Loose incense is the best to use, particularly if it has been blended for the specific purpose of circle-, divination- or meditation-work.

Blends commonly comprise gums such as frankincense, myrrh, copal or benzoin; a base such as white or

It is now common for people to have oil burners at home.

A supply of bottles and droppers are very useful aids to blending oils.

red sandalwood; dried herbs, flowers and/or berries; and occasionally essential oils or even store-cupboard ingredients such as honey, dried fruit or wine. For blending, you will need a clean working surface such as a marble chopping board, a pestle and mortar and some jars for storage. A sharp knife, or better still a double-handled herb chopper, is a real boon for preparation.

The benefit of using loose incense is that you can create special blends suited to the particular purposes of the ritual work you are undertaking.

Different blends can be created for different Moon phases and Sabbats, as well as blends for elemental work and specific types of spells. The blends should be created at the appropriate Moon phase in order to capture the energies you wish to release when the incense is burned. The loose blends are burned on a red-hot charcoal disc, which can be purchased at alternative shops and over the internet. These discs are placed in fire-proof censers which in turn are placed on a fire-proof mat to prevent scorch damage to floors and furniture.

LOVE-INCENSE

This love blend can be used for the ritual of Handfasting (see pages 168–169), and should be lit prior to casting the circle.

For the best results, the incense should be made when the Moon is waxing.

Blend all the ingredients to draw love.

½ teaspoon powdered orris root

1 teaspoon rose petals

½ teaspoon myrrh

1 teaspoon honeysuckle

½ teaspoon white sandalwood

½ teaspoon honey

1 teaspoon chopped raisins

Caution

If you are pregnant, have high blood pressure or suffer from any serious health problems, you are strongly advised to consult a medical practitioner or therapist before using any oils or incense ingredients.

All essential oils need to be diluted before they can be used on the skin or in the bath; some essential oils are not appropriate for use in this way. These very powerful essences have physical effects and should be treated with great respect.

Diluted oil for anointing objects or persons should never be more concentrated than seven drops of essential oil to one tablespoon of carrier oil (grapeseed, almond or olive oil), and care should be taken at all times to keep oil away from the eyes.

GREEN WITCHCRAFT

It should be obvious by now that Wiccans have a very special bond with nature and the environment. This relationship is one of reverence and responsibility; we cannot venerate the spirit of nature while ignoring the often adverse impact that humans have on our environment. Many of us perceive the Earth-web – the connected strands that link all beings and elements on the planet – as a whole being. Sometimes we call this interconnected bio-system 'Gaia', after the primal Earth-mother who gave birth pathenogenically (without insemination) to the Waters, the Sky and the Mountains.

Whether we believe in Gaia as a unitary entity or as a symbol of the interdependence of all beings on the planet, we feel responsible for the wellbeing of the Earth. Gaia as a system is in trouble and so are we. The expanding hole in the ozone layer, the rapid changes in our weather systems and rise in global temperatures all signal danger. We know what we need to do: move towards biodegradability; quit burning fossil fuels and destroying the rain forests; stop pumping wastes into the air, the earth and the water; find safe, sustainable forms of energy.

We rely on the survival of the Earth; the health of the planet is important to everyone. As witches, we derive our powers and nourish our spiritual selves through contact with the natural world. Watching our planet home being polluted is very

On planet Earth we are all 'relations' – people, trees, rivers, animals and birds.

distressing. Seeing our fellow beings – trees, fields and rivers, animals and birds – facing destruction is extremely difficult. All of these beings are our 'relations'; for witches, they are neighbours and friends with whom we seek to co-exist.

PRACTICAL ACTION

Because we are practical people, this action means we must do more than stand in circles casting healing spells for the planet. Consequently, most witches have a very involved approach towards saving the Earth. This may take the form of practical, collective activity, such as neighbourhood litter collection, beach clearances, reclaiming and planting abandoned patches or lots in the locality, or broader, more overtly political activity such as protests, petitions or other contributions to environmental campaigns. This is in addition to organizing our own households so that we conserve water, recycle paper, cans and glass, and shop responsibly for environmentally friendly products.

One very positive activity that many witches get involved with is tree planting. Not only does this provide good exercise and get us outdoors, it can often be instructive, especially when meeting people with a great deal of knowledge and experience of the natural environment. It is not unusual, on a tree-planting mission,

to combine planting with a ritual or blessing for the trees we are bedding-in. This encourages us to remember the bond we share with all our relations and helps us to link with the Earth and its growth cycles.

Witches see the natural world as a magical place. When we drum on sea-shores, chant in the woods or dance around standing stones that our ancestors used to mark the passage of the stars and planets, we find ways to harmonize with the spirits of nature. However, we are all deeply aware that drumming, chanting and dancing alone are not enough, and that in order to save the environment, we have to take responsibility and act accordingly.

Taking responsibility for the Earth means practical involvement.

THE
EIGHT SABBATS

THE YEAR'S WHEEL

Our ancestors acknowledged the human relationship with the Earth's seasonal round by marking particular points in the year's turning with celebrations. The remnants of many folk customs indicate the importance placed upon human interconnectedness with nature, the flow and ebb of the tides and seasons of Earth's solar revolution. In Wicca, the strands of these customs have been reclaimed and woven into the eight festivals of the Wiccan year, which are known widely as the Sabbats.

THE EIGHT SABBATS

Festival	Northern Hemisphere	Southern Hemisphere
Samhain	31 October	1 May
Yule (winter solstice)	21/22 December	21/22 June
Imbolc	1/2 February	1/2 August
Ostara (spring equinox)	21/22 March	21/22 September
Beltane	1 May	31 October
Litha (summer solstice)	21/22 June	21/22 December
Lughnasadh	1/2 August	1/2 February
Modron (autumn equinox)	21/22 September	21/22 March

The winter solstice marks both stillness and change.

Of the eight festivals that witches celebrate through the year, four of them are based directly on the astronomical events produced by Gaia's 23.45° tilt: the winter and summer solstices and the spring and autumn equinoxes. The dates of the eight Sabbat festivals of the northern hemisphere are reversed in the southern hemisphere (see box opposite). This takes account of the fact that countries in the southern hemisphere experience winter while those in the northern experience summer, and so on.

THE SOLAR FESTIVALS

Each of the four solar festivals has a special name in Wiccan tradition. The winter solstice is known as Yule and comes from a Scandinavian word *Yul* meaning 'wheel'. We assume that our Nordic ancestors perceived this as a time of stillness and completion – a point on the turning wheel of the year that completed a cycle. The summer solstice is known as Litha and the origin of this word is more obscure. Strangely, it is also thought to mean 'wheel', although perhaps for

Some festivals are marked by nature's changes rather than by the calendar.

altogether different reasons (see pages 60–61). The spring or vernal equinox is sometimes called the 'Festival of Trees' and is best known in Wicca as Ostara. The festival is named after a Teutonic goddess of fertility (in Anglo-Saxon *Eostre*), and celebrates the return of growth and new birth to the Earth. The autumn equinox is known to Wiccans as Modron, which means 'mother'. Modron is considered to be the All-Mother, the fertile, fecund and nurturing aspect of the Goddess, appropriate to the season of fruitfulness.

If we imagine the year as a wheel, with Yule in the north and Litha in the south (reverse in the southern hemisphere), the other two solar festivals are planted squarely on the perpendicular. Crosswise to these, and intersecting each of the solar festivals, are the four Sabbats known as the Celtic fire festivals. Although roughly attached to calendar dates, these are slightly more movable feasts and some witches prefer to mark these when particular plants appear or the first appropriate lunation thereafter, usually the first Full Moon.

CELTIC FIRE FESTIVALS

The first of these festivals, moving around the wheel from east to west starting at the winter solstice, is Imbolc (pronounced im-molk), meaning 'ewe's milk'. Traditionally, this is the festival celebrated when the first snowdrops appear or the first Full Moon thereafter (see dates for both hemispheres in the box on page 44). The festival has strong associations with the Celtic fire goddess Brighid (pronounced breed), sometimes called Brigit or Bride/Bridie, and is often called the Feast of Brighid. Imbolc marks the quickening of the Earth, the first thaws after winter, the birth of the lambs and the first signs that spring is coming.

Continuing around the wheel, between Ostara and Litha, is Beltane (pronounced either bell-tayne or bile-tin), meaning 'bright fire'. Beltane is celebrated when the first May-blossom blooms or on the first Full Moon thereafter (see dates for both hemispheres in the box on page 44). Beltane celebrates the greening of the Earth and all aspects of fertility in vegetation, birds and animals. This festival is associated with the Green Man, a spirit or god of nature,

The pagan festivals mark the rhythms of nature.

The cycle of life, death and renewal can be seen all around us.

depictions of which are abundant throughout Britain.

Between Litha and Modron comes the festival of Lughnasadh (pronounced loo-na-sah) or Lammas, celebrated when the first corn sheaf is cut or the first Full Moon after that (see dates for both hemispheres in the box on page 44). Lughnasadh celebrates the cereal harvest and the gathering in of blessings and honours the spirit of plenty that brings the corn to ripeness.

Finally, between Modron and Yule is the Sabbat known as Samhain (pronounced sow-ain) meaning 'first frost'. As its name suggests, this is sometimes celebrated when the

It is an old tradition, for the Celtic fire festivals at least, that the festival begins at sundown the day before and ends on the following sundown. This means that if you celebrate Beltane on 1 May, the festival actually begins at sundown on 30 April.

PAGAN SPIRITUALITY

Exploring the customs and the meanings of the various festivals will help you to understand more about pagan spirituality. Experiencing for yourself the way that witches work with Gaia's many tides and seasons will also help you to attune to the spirit of nature and understand better the changes and shifts that occur in your own life.

You will find that each Sabbat is a still moment that we create on a wheel that represents a constant state of flux. Litha celebrates the longest day of the year, but carries within it the message that the hours of daylight will afterwards diminish. The spring equinox brings a perfect balance of light with darkness, but thereafter we tip over into the season of greatest light. The same is true of all the solar festivals, and at a more subtle level, the Celtic fire festivals. Each marks events in the Earth's seasonal cycle and each carries the seeds of its own demise. You will learn for yourself the deeper spiritual lessons that the Sabbats impart as you follow the cycle around.

first frosts come, or on the first Full Moon thereafter (see dates for both hemispheres in the box on page 44). This is the Feast of the Ancestors, the Day of the Dead and also the old Celtic New Year. It also marks a time where we leave the warmer days of autumn behind us and go down into the darkness that will lead us back to Yule.

SAMHAIN – THE FESTIVAL OF THE DEAD

Celebrated on the last day of October in the northern hemisphere and the first day of May in the southern, Samhain stands halfway between the autumn equinox Modron and Yule. It is sometimes seen as the beginning of winter, but it is also the Festival of the Dead, when we remember and honour the ancestors. It is a magical time when the veil between the worlds of the dead and the living is thin, and in Wicca we celebrate death as a part of life, and to give positive value to the idea of going into the dark.

NEW BEGINNINGS

Our Celtic ancestors saw Samhain as a key point of the year's turning and a chance to begin anew. The eighth-century scholarly monk Bede noted that custom named November as the 'blood month' and he attributed the name to the fact that this is the time of slaughtering beasts in preparation for winter provisions.

With the surplus from summer burned on a 'balefire', our peace made with the dead and preparations for the winter well under way, our ancestors are likely to have seen this as a key departure point from the old cycle into the new. This is why pagans today refer to this festival as the Celtic New Year. Although Samhain literally means 'first frost', and is thus the first of the winter festivals, it also marks preparation for change.

Pumpkins are often used to create lantern 'faces' for the Samhain festivals.

This is the season of the Hag Goddess, associated with nocturnal creatures.

CELEBRATING THE CRONE GODDESS

The season is associated with ghosts, spirits and the dead walking. It is the season of the Hag or *Calliach* (Scots Gaelic meaning 'old woman'), the crone aspect of the Goddess who midwives us, with great compassion, from life to death. She is Rhiannon, goddess of transition, Ceridwen, goddess of the cauldron of transformation, and Hecate, weaver of wisdom and guardian at the crossroads. The Crone Goddess is celebrated to some extent in the plastic masks and costumes that children wear at Hallowe'en.

Nowadays, witches celebrate the crone goddess by holding a ritual in which we name, honour, remember and speak with the dead. Beginning with those who have died in the last year, we move on to family and friends and then commemorate all our ancestors. Then, out of grief, we bring back joy and name the newborn babies of the last year, the new friends and opportunities we have met.

The festival of Samhain serves as a reminder not only that life contains death, but also that it contains the mystery of rebirth and the movement of the cycle ever onwards.

YULE – THE WINTER SOLSTICE

Sometimes called midwinter, Yule marks the shortest day and, since the worst days of winter are usually to follow, is more accurately 'mid-year'. The sixteenth-century poet John Donne called this time 'The year's midnight', when 'The world's whole sap is sunk'. However, Yule carries within it a paradox – just as the winter solstice commemorates the annual demise of the Sun's powers, it witnesses its rebirth. This is why Yule is also known as 'Sun-return'.

Yule is the time when the Goddess labours to bring forth the Star Child, and in fact Yule was called 'Mothernight' by our northern European ancestors. For witches who celebrate God and Goddess, this is the Solar God who, by the time of Ostara, will grow into the young man who impregnates the young, fertile aspect of the Goddess, and another Star Child who will succeed him the following Yule.

The winter solstice is a time of repose and rebirth.

The holly is the sacred plant of protection.

SOLAR REBIRTH

However we see it, the symbolism of this solar rebirth is mirrored in our celebrations. At the darkest time, when the Earth seems bare and forlorn, we bring evergreens into our homes – holly for protection, ivy for the faithful promise that life endures, mistletoe for fertility. In the first days of winter, these remind us that Earth will be green again.

We feast to lighten our hearts and share the fellowship of others to warm ourselves from within when all around seems bleak. The importance to us of human company at Yule is evident in the numbers who travel to sacred sites to witness sunrise or sunset together. Members of my own group organize a community ceilidh – a social gathering with folk music and dance – to celebrate Yule and bring some of its message to everyone in our local community.

Although the surface of the Earth is denuded of its most luxurious greenery in the dark season, below the surface seeds are sleeping, ready for germination. Witches take their cue from this to use the darkest time to delve into the deeper places of our minds and spirits, to meditate and bring back new ideas, projects and developments in our lives. In our rituals to mark Yule, we look for the invisible Sun; the vital inner spark which, re-energized, will keep our spirits and our physical energy going through the winter. The candles we light to rekindle the fires of Sol also symbolize our desire to relight our inner Sun. 'As above; so below', as the Wise say.

IMBOLC – THE FEAST OF BRIGHID

By Imbolc the days are noticeably longer and signs that winter is loosening its grip can be seen. The first shoots are pushing through the soil and snowdrops, the 'Maids of February', are gracing gardens and woodlands. Imbolc marks the birth of the first lambs and the ewes begin to lactate; hence the association of the festival with milking. In one old song, 'Ailse Ban', a milkmaid soothes the cow she is milking by assuring her that 'the Holy St Bridget' herself is milking 'the white *kye* (clouds) in heaven'.

The 'St Bridget' in question is a Christianized version of the Irish fire goddess Brighid, whose immense popularity could not be eradicated by Christianity. Even among pagans today, Brighid is a much-beloved goddess, and Imbolc is seen as her festival. Brighid's role as fierce protector of women, children and newborn animals is reflected in Christian mythology, where St Bridget is the reputed midwife to Mary. In Wicca, she is midwife to the spring, the divine woman who breathes her fiery breath upon the Earth to awaken it. Her role extends to enabling new projects – many of us plant seeds and bulbs at this time to represent areas in our lives that we wish to nurture and grow.

Imbolc marks the emergence of the first snowdrops.

SECRET RITES

Imbolc is very much a women's festival, and, traditionally, for the first part of the celebration, women practise their own rites which are never spoken of outside the circle or when men are present. The men, of course, have their own mysteries to practise while they wait to be invited into the circle as honoured guests. They bring gifts for Brighid, which are laid at the feet of a *bridiog* – an effigy of the goddess which is dressed and decorated by the women and placed in a basket. Throughout the ritual, celebrants may approach the *bridiog* to whisper to her their own specific secrets and wishes.

Brighid is a goddess of healing, inspiration of poets and patron of blacksmiths and metalworkers. She is the fire in the head of poets and the fire in the belly of those who act upon their ideas – a goddess of inspiration and action. As patron of metalworkers, she is the key to turning raw materials into useful and beautiful things – a goddess of transformation. At Imbolc, a time of renewal, we celebrate changes around and within us, and renew our commitment to making the world a better place. We honour the spark of divine creativity within us and raise healing energy.

This Chalice Well at Chalice Well garden in Glastonbury, England.

OSTARA – THE VERNAL EQUINOX

Ostara marks the vernal (meaning youthful) equinox – a time of balance between daylight and darkness, the point before day is longer than night. It falls in the Christian season of Lent in the northern hemisphere (see the box on page 44 for dates in the southern hemisphere), which itself comes from an Anglo-Saxon word, referring to the 'lengthening' of the days.

The festival of Ostara is also a celebration of growth and derives its name from a German goddess whose totem was the hare.

We are all familiar with the saying, 'Mad as a March hare'. It comes from observations of their mating behaviour at this time of year, as the animals appear to 'box' and leap about in the fields. In fact, hares are no more crazy in their behaviour in March than at any other time of the year; it is just that the grass is still short enough in March for their antics to be visible! The hare is seen as prolifically fertile and many Moon goddesses linked with women's reproductive cycles share it as a totem of earthy sexuality and fecundity. Today's Easter Bunny is a bowdlerized descendant of this early pagan fertility symbol, but is nonetheless regarded with fondness by witches who recognize it as a modern remnant of a cherished ancient tradition.

SYMBOL OF FERTILITY AND RENEWAL

Eggs have been linked with this time of year for thousands of years. This enduring, pre-Christian symbol of fertility, renewal and the life-force inspires pagans today to celebrate by decorating eggs for the Ostara celebrations. Sometimes these hollow, painted eggs are hung on a branch placed in the centre of our sacred spaces. This is a branch

The hare is considered sacred to the goddess of the Moon.

Eggs represent fertility and potential.

thrown by the winter or early spring winds and should never be cut from a living tree. As the eggs represent 'life-in-potential', we magically imbue them with wishes we hope will manifest during the coming summer.

Ostara is a good time to be out in nature and witness for ourselves the effects of the sap rising in the trees, the buds and the busy behaviour of nesting birds. It is a time to visit the daffodils – the flower of this festival – in their natural setting, and discover why they are called harbingers of spring. It is also an ideal time to seek balance in our own lives; in our celebrations, we sometimes walk between a black candle and a white one, and pause before we pass through this gateway into summer, to ask the God or Goddess what we can do to restore the balance in our lives that will enable us to grow.

BELTANE – THE TIME OF THE GREEN MAN

The feast of Beltane celebrates the coming of summer. It is the time when we honour the Green Man, consort of the Goddess and ancient spirit of the Greenwood. Known as 'Jack-in-the-Green' or 'Robin', he joins with Marian at this time, his May Queen.

Hal an tow, jolly rumble oh

We were up long before the day oh

To welcome in the summer

To welcome in the may oh

The summer is a-comin' in

And winter's gone away oh

'Hal-an-Tow':
Trad. English Maying Song

sexual licence, so possibly 'bringing in the May' was a euphemism for a more traditional activity of Beltane. Unsurprisingly, many pagan handfastings and marriages take place at this festival.

Maypoles are ancient symbols of fertility.

This is the season of Herne, protector of the Greenwood and symbol of fertility, growth and change. Just as buck deer shed their antlers following mating in May, with the Goddess pregnant with the Star Child, Herne declares his readiness to forsake his wanderings and take his place beside her. On Beltane Eve, some witches take to the woods, to 'bring in' the May-blossom at dawn. For our ancestors, this was a time of

CLOSE TO THE FAERY WORLD

In the wheel of the year, the festival of Beltane stands opposite that of Samhain; just as at Samhain when the veil between the worlds of the living and the dead is thin, at Beltane the world of mortals and that of faery are very close. The faery Otherworld was well-known by our ancestors, who left us stories of seers and poets who gained their gifts after falling asleep under a hawthorn, May-tree or faery-mound.

Our Celtic ancestors drove cattle between two sacred fires on 1 May to protect them before sending them out to pasture; this was the bel-tine, the 'lucky' or 'bright' fire. The feast may also be named after a northern European god or goddess named Bel/Belenos/Belissama. The Celtic preface bel translates as 'bright', indicating that this god or goddess had solar connections.

Fires set at Beltane are intended to bring luck and blessings.

Whatever the festival's origins, the sacred fire features strongly in Wiccan celebrations. If celebrating outdoors, we light a small bonfire which the sprightly among us can leap to obtain a Beltane blessing. Sometimes a broomstick is used instead, symbolizing the sacred conjunction of male (handle) and female (brush), and marking the threshold between spring and summer. As we cross either fire or broomstick, we make promises to keep in the coming year.

THE SUMMER SOLSTICE

Although the best of summer is usually yet to come, the summer solstice marks the height of the Sun's powers on the longest day of the year. This is the time to gather strength from the Sun before the hours of daylight begin to diminish over the next six months. Like Yule, the festival of Litha carries within it a paradox; the moment we celebrate the Sun's powers at their greatest is the very moment those powers begin to wane. This reminds us of an essential physical and spiritual truth – that our festivals are fleeting instants of stillness on the wheel of change and are themselves symbols of the constant flux that is the nature of all existence.

ANCIENT TRADITIONS

The word Litha is supposed to mean 'wheel', though its origins are obscure. There may be a link, however, with a custom first recorded two thousand years ago, of setting a wheel alight and rolling it downhill, representing, presumably, the fall of the Sun at the height of its powers. There might also have been an element of sympathetic magic here; symbolically sending the Sun down to warm the fields and thus urge the growth of the crops in the coming season. Certainly there is a strong association with fire at midsummer – which, like Yule, is more accurately termed 'mid-year' with the best of the weather yet to come.

The Hele Stone at Stonehenge in Wiltshire, England, marks the point of sunrise on the summer solstice.

Bonfires have been lit and torches carried around hillsides at this time for at least the last seven centuries, and one suspects for much earlier, before written records of these practices were made.

CELEBRATING LITHA

Litha is usually celebrated out of doors, weather permitting, and witches tend to gather at the old sacred sites – the standing stones, circles and hillsides – in order to observe the solstice sunrise with others. Many of us set off on the evening of 20 June (20 December in the southern hemisphere, see page 44) to keep vigil together until sunrise on the next day. This means staying awake during the shortest night, and keeping each other entertained with stories and songs after drumming the sun down below the horizon at sunset. At dawn, we begin drumming again, this time to encourage old Sol's exertions to rise early, ride high and shine long and bright upon the longest day of the year. The rest of the day is usually spent outside, sharing rituals and food, catching up on lost sleeping – and getting home

LUGHNASADH – THE HARVEST FESTIVAL

Lughnasadh falls between the summer solstice, when the Sun's strength is greatest, and the autumn equinox, when daylight and darkness are of equal length. It celebrates the cereal harvest and its alternative name, Lammas, is thought to come from the Anglo-Saxon *Hlaef-mass* meaning 'loaf mass'. The title 'Lughnasadh', however, derives from the name of the Irish God Lugh whom contemporary pagans honour as a Sun deity, and this harvest festival marks the gathering in of the grains ripened by his or her rays.

For our ancient ancestors, the cycle of cereal crops represented something altogether more mysterious; the growth, fall and rebirth of the grain reflected the human cycle of birth, death and continuation. Carvings representing corn can be found in ancient burial sites, indicating its spiritual as well as its material significance. The spirit of the corn had to be propitiated and tempted back to the fields, and it is known from documented customs of more recent centuries that a couple would make love in a field shorn of corn in order to enact the regeneration of the crops. The mysterious but potent corn spirit was lured into and captured by the woven corn dollies that feature at this festival, also known as 'spirit cages'.

This is the time of 'John Barleycorn', the caring father aspect of the god who was wedded to the pregnant Goddess in May, and is now cut down as the harvest, to feed the people. Some witches see the harvest as a gift from the Mother Goddess, who shares her body to nourish

Corn dollies represent the spirit of the corn.

The blessings of the harvest are celebrated at Lughnasadh.

her children. Again we see one of the contradictions innate within the festivals; the time of plenty and celebration is also the time of cutting down and sacrifice. Lammas fairs still exist in parts of England, remnants of a time when the cereal harvest was greeted with great jubilation.

It is hard for city-dwellers, who have the privilege of the year-round availability of nutritious food, to understand the importance of the harvest to people for whom the staple stock from last year may have run out many weeks before. At Lammas, the time of gathering in the blessings we reap from the planting, we are reminded also of the importance of its distribution. Consequently, some witches combine their enjoyment of feasting and celebrating this time of plenty with a commitment to 'giving back' either through charitable or political work, to ensure a fair harvest for all.

MODRON – THE AUTUMNAL EQUINOX

At the west of the year's compass stands Modron, like Ostara a day when daylight and darkness are of equal length. Unlike Ostara, however, which brings the promise of longer days, the autumn equinox foreshadows the darker days to come. Modron is the harvest of the fruits of the Earth Mother, who in her aspect as eternal Goddess enters the third trimester of her pregnancy. For witches who honour God and Goddess, this is the time when the dying Sun God begins his journey across the western ocean to sojourn with the eldest aspect of the Goddess, in the land of the dead at Samhain.

Witches can see within the Arthurian legends echoes of the dying god in the fallen King Arthur, who is borne westwards towards either the Summerlands or Avalon, the Celtic Otherworld, accompanied by three, sometimes nine maidens, thought to symbolize the triple Goddess. His renewal is seen in the birth of the Star Child at the winter solstice and his rapid growth to youth, hero and protector in the next year's cycle.

THE MYSTERY WITHIN

The connection between Avalon – the 'Isle of Apples' – and Modron continues with some of the celebrations of the Modron festival today. In our rituals, we slice open apples to reveal the mystery within – a five-pointed star symbolizing all elements of life combined. We eat these apples to remind ourselves that, as witches, we walk between two worlds; that of consensual reality and that of the magical Otherworld. At this festival, we stand between the pillars of light and darkness, ready to descend, with all those goddesses whose myths are associated with the

Apple trees are thought to mark boundaries between the worlds.

Modron is the year's sunset.

Underworld, into the long night of the year. We eat the fruits of liminality, and like Inanna, Persephone, Freya and Ishtar, prepare ourselves for the descent into the deep, creative darkness of the six months to follow. Just as seeds germinate in the darkness of the rich earth, we continue to grow by preparing ourselves for stillness in the dark, reaching into the deep places of regeneration within, and bringing back the treasures of creativity and spiritual knowledge when, at last, we return.

If Yule is the year's midnight, Modron is its sunset and in this dusk we carry what we can of the Sun's noon-day strength at Litha with us into the dark. After Modron we continue towards Samhain, and having travelled the sacred wheel of the year, continue the cycle around.

THE FIVE
SACRED ELEMENTS

THE ELEMENTS

In Classical Greece, where philosophy, physics and religion were indivisible, our pagan ancestors believed that all material existence in the Universe was divided into five separate elements. These were the elements of Air, Fire, Water and Earth. The fifth was various postulated as 'Love', 'Aether' or 'Quintessence'. Various cultures have at different times marked similar distinctions between the elements of life. The European Celts, for example, honoured three sacred elements, Earth, Fire and Water, represented by the 'triskeles', the three-armed symbols found carved at ancient sites.

Witches today honour the five sacred elements of which the Universe is composed: Air, Fire, Water, Earth and Spirit. Although these can be seen in their raw form – Air as the gas we breathe, Fire as flame, Water as H_2O, Earth as rock – these first four elements are also experienced as components of complex forms. A tree, for example, is composed of Earth (soil, plant matter), Water (sap and tapped moisture), Fire (photosynthesis and the heat that initiates growth and regeneration), and Air (it creates oxygen from carbon dioxide).

The fifth element, Spirit – that which connects all things – causes the first four elements to conjoin in particular proportions and forms to produce life and the Universe as we experience it. Spirit is the sacred weaver of the elements and as 'the connection' is,

The five sacred elements are Air, Fire, Water, Earth and Spirit. Together, they are the basis of all existence.

Water covers most of our planet's surface.

along with the other four, an equal cause and part of the Universe. It is also the great web of life that joins all beings to each other.

ACCESSING THE DIVINE WITHIN

Although life around us exemplifies the combination of the elements, we separate these out in ritual and magic to symbolize and honour the sacred life-force that forms all of existence. Symbolism is a key principle of Wiccan spirituality and magical tradition. In a culture where rationality rules, sometimes we need to by-pass our conscious, sensible, rational selves by appealing to our instinctive selves, in order to tap into the deep spiritual well within. This 'deep' level is the divine within us, the umbilical by which we are joined to the sum of the divine, the Goddess. The instinctive self responds to symbols, and these are the gateway to the world of the 'semiotic' or 'Goddess space', the primordial space-time of spirit and magic.

THE SYMBOLISM OF THE ELEMENTS

Element	Direction	Colour	Associated Human Trait
Air	East	Yellow	Rational thought
Fire	South	Red	Willpower, courage
Water	West	Blue	Emotions
Earth	North	Green	Physicality
Spirit	Centre	Purple or white	

Finding new ways to see and feel Air aids visualization.

Accordingly, when witches work ritual and magic in sacred space, we symbolize the elemental aspects of the material Universe in order to draw upon them in the transformational work we are undertaking.

For witches, the symbolism of the five elements, the fundamental stuff of life itself, is of primary importance. Whenever witches work in sacred space (see pages 116–125) we invoke the elements, asking them to bring their gifts and energies to support our magical work. We set Air, Fire, Water and Earth in the four sacred directions; the cardinal points of the compass – east, south, west and north respectively – with Spirit at the centre of the circle.

It is important to remember that the elements are a physical reality, as well as part of a magical and spiritual system of symbols. Their physical manifestation is the very basis of spiritual and magical work. We breathe Air and its movement carries plant spores and aids pollination, as do the birds that wing through it. Fire is the warmth and light of the Sun, without which there would be no life on this planet. Water covers over three-fifths of the Earth's surface and our evolutionary ancestors crawled out from it onto dry land. Earth is rock, stone, soil, the nourishment of the vegetation that it supports. Spirit is in the life-giving connections we see all around us, much in the way that we perceive the effects of love, but never its separate, physical essence; it is the most mysterious and wonderful of the elements.

For witches, the five elements are the basis of all existence. We express their sacred nature in the sign of the pentacle, the upright five-pointed star in a circle. Within this symbol, the elements of Air, Fire, Water, Earth and Spirit are joined by one single unbroken line, encompassed by the sacred circle of life that has no beginning and no ending. The very fact that so many witches wear the pentacle as a sign of pagan spirituality demonstrates the importance with which the elements are regarded within the Craft.

Working with Earth helps you connect with your natural surroundings.

AIR

Air represents communication, reason and memory. In sacred space, the eastern segment for this element is often decorated in yellow, with wind-chimes, feathers, carved birds, airborne seeds, scented herbs such as lavender or mint, and wands. It may include symbols or depictions of deities we associate with Air: Athena, goddess of wisdom; or Hermes (Mercury), god of swiftness and communication. We burn incense at this quarter of the sacred circle, as Air is the element of scent.

When we invoke Air, we are not merely invoking an element external to ourselves, but one that resides within us. It is important, therefore, to work towards building a relationship with Air at a physical as well as a symbolic level.

THE PROPERTIES OF AIR

The symbolic functions of Air are concerned with reason, learning, intellectual knowledge, communication, the law, movement, expedition and language. The physical gifts of Air are breath, the wind, sound, scent and memory. It is invisible, but can be felt around us. Collect symbols that encapsulate the element of Air and work with Air through your breath-work, meditating on your chosen symbols and conscious contact with Air in the natural world.

Ritual staffs and wands symbolize air.

WORKING WITH AIR

1 Set aside some time alone to focus on your breath. Relax and deliberately slow your breathing down. Take a deep breath into your lungs through your nostrils, hold for as long as is comfortable and expel through your mouth. Repeat three times.

2 Imagine the next breath is your first ever; hold and as you breathe out, imagine it is your last. How does it feel? Try to remember a time when your breathing was impeded, perhaps by a cold. What did this feel like?

3 Take a deep breath and make a moaning sound as you breathe out, changing the sound by the shape of your mouth, constricting your throat and re-positioning your tongue. Now try to form word-sounds without expelling breath. Take note of what happens when you do this.

4 Take a walk on a windy day. How does the speed and power of the air's movement affect the landscape around you? What do you hear as you walk? What do you smell and feel?

RITUAL WELCOME TO AIR

Officer for Air:
In the east, the element of Air; communication, reason and memory, our first breath and our last, you are honoured in this circle. Be present at our rites and bring to this circle your gifts of clarity, teaching, learning and understanding.

Officer lights a yellow candle in the east:
Hail and welcome!

All:
Hail and welcome!

FIRE

Fire represents inspiration, passion and courage. In ritual space, the Fire quarter is often decorated in red, with candles, lamps, carved dragons or salamanders, flowers and associated herbs, spices and gums such as frankincense, cinnamon, cactus or coriander, and athames (witches' knives) or swords. Symbols or images of deities associated with Fire may be included: Brighid, Celtic fire goddess or Belenos, god of the Sun. We burn lamps and candles in the south of our circles as physical representations of Fire.

In order to summon our inner Fire, we need to connect with and understand its function in the physical Universe as well as within Wiccan symbolism. This requires a little time set aside to consider the element in all its aspects and to experience its material function in our own lives.

UNDERSTANDING FIRE

The symbolic functions of Fire are inspiration, willpower, courage, activity and energy, and empowerment. The physical gifts of Fire are flame, combustion, electricity, warmth and light, body-heat and the rays of the Sun. Assemble some symbols that represent Fire and continue working with it through your conscious contact with its various forms in everyday life.
Spend some time to meditate on your chosen symbols.

Lights symbolize light as a gift of Fire.

WORKING WITH FIRE

1 Walk through a park or town on a sunny day. Become conscious of the warmth of the Sun on your face, and the light that penetrates your closed eyelids.

2 How are the people, animals or plants around you affected by the light and heat of the Sun?

3 Another form of Fire is electricity. In mild weather, if you are at home alone, turn off all but strictly essential sources of electricity for one evening. Spend the evening in candlelight, without TV or music. If you can, light a bonfire outside.

4 How does the lack of electricity affect your activities? What do you experience with the different forms of fire you are using to create light and heat?

Blades often represent Fire.

RITUAL WELCOME TO FIRE

Officer for Fire:
In the south, the element of Fire; inspiration, passion and courage, the spark that ignited our existence, you are honoured in this circle. Be present at our rites and bring to this circle your gifts of willpower, daring and creativity.

Officer lights a red candle in the south:
Hail and welcome!

All:
Hail and welcome!

WATER

Water represents intuition, dreams and emotions. In our rituals, the Water quarter is often decorated in blue, with glass pebbles, depictions of sea-creatures, 'watery' herbs and flowers such as roses, hyacinths, myrtle and lovage, and a chalice. We may add symbols or images of Water-associated deities, such as Rhiannon, Welsh goddess of rebirth, or Yemana, Santeria goddess of the sea. Working with the element of Water involves having direct knowledge of the vital purpose it serves in our physical environment as well as understanding its symbolic nature and meaning.

In order to 'connect' with Water, set aside time to find out more about it and experience for yourself its physical impact on our daily lives.

In the circle the chalice is the symbol for water.

Waterways are the arteries of the planet.

The spiritual significance of Water is balance, healing, love and the emotions, mystery, birth, women's cycles and arcane knowledge. Its physical gifts are cleansing, life-giving moisture, cooling, quenching and the blood and fluids of our bodies. In order to continue your work with Water, gather and meditate on symbols that represent this element, and build a more conscious awareness of Water's everyday physical functions.

WORKING WITH WATER

1 Take yourself off to a beach or the shore of a tidal sea, river or lake, and walk along the edge of the water at low tide. Walk with your eyes cast down towards the ground and watch the movement of the water as it ebbs and flows. Consider the rhythm of the water.

2 What do you see when the tide goes out? How has the water affected the form of the landscape? Observe the other humans on the shore. What are they doing? Where are they looking? What attracts humans to the waterside?

3 If you live near the coast, research your local tides in the library or on the internet. Visit the sea to observe how tides change from high tide to low tide.

4 Set aside time to meditate on what you have seen; close your eyes and place the index finger of your left hand on the bone on the inside of your right wrist on your pulse. How does it feel to know that you carry rivers, streams and tributaries inside you? What function do streams and rivers serve on our planet?

RITUAL WELCOME TO WATER

Officer for Water:
In the west, the element of Water; intuition, dreams and emotions, seas, rain, rivers and the primordial waters of birth, you are honoured in this circle. Be present at our rites and bring to this circle your gifts of love, balance and healing.

Officer lights a blue candle in the west:
Hail and welcome!

All:
Hail and welcome!

EARTH

Earth represents fertility, stability and practicality. In Wicca, the Earth quarter is usually decorated in green, and contains living plants, wood, crystals and stones, fallen branches and images of forest creatures, 'earthy' herbs, gums and oils such as patchouli, cypress, yew or mandrake, and a pentacle. We may include images of appropriate deities such as the Greek goddess, Demeter, the harvest goddess or the Green Man. The element of Earth – matter – is the basis of the physical Universe.

Working with Earth requires an understanding of its physical nature and experience of the importance of 'matter' on our planet. Its presence is most obvious to us in the spectacular side of nature; in mountain ranges and canyons, earthquakes or erupting volcanoes. But it is evident in less dramatic ways, in our everyday experience. It forms the matter and bones of our own bodies, the ground on which we walk, and feeds the vegetation that keeps our planet green and living.

The spiritual properties of Earth are manifestation, fruition, fertility, embodiment and solidity. Its physical gifts are sensation, physicality, food, shelter and the shield of protection. Build your connection with Earth by continuing to experience and meditate on its physical properties and gather symbols that represent its physical and spiritual gifts.

Mountains are the bones of the planet.

WORKING WITH EARTH

1 Set aside some time to go out into a local natural landscape. What shapes it and which species of plants and animals make their homes there? While you move, become conscious of the different textures that the surface of the ground yields.

2 Meditate on your own 'earthliness'. Close your eyes, and sitting or standing on the ground's surface, imagine yourself melding to the floor, becoming one with the deep layers of soil, rock, roots and bones that extend beneath you.

3 Now rise and keep within yourself the image of your Earth-form. Remember the feeling of melding to the floor as you begin to walk, slowly at first. You have become a moving mountain. Think about how that feels as you take each new step.

4 Now touch the outline of your own body. Think of yourself as a mountain range that is physically separate from and yet interdependent on the Earth. Have you thought of your Earth connection in such a way before?

RITUAL WELCOME TO EARTH

Officer for Earth:
In the north, the element of Earth; fertility, stability and practicality, rock, crystal, soil, bones and body, you are honoured in this circle. Be present at our rites and bring to this circle your gifts of sheltered protection and manifestation.

Officer lights a green candle in the north:
Hail and welcome!

All:
Hail and welcome!

SPIRIT

Spirit represents connection, magic and transformation. Called Ether in some Wiccan traditions, Spirit is set in the centre of the ritual space which we decorate in purple or white. We use spider and web symbols and totems denoting divine 'magical' patrons such as Hecate or Changing Woman, and decorate with quartz crystals, threads and distaffs. Working with the element of Spirit requires an understanding of its function within our everyday lives, which calls for imagination and a willingness to set aside preconceived ideas.

Spirit – connection – is the soul of formation and interdependence. Because it weaves irrevocable change, it is often expressed as transformation. As with love or courage, we recognize its effects rather than a separate, physical presence. Spirit oversees and takes part in the birth and death of stars. It is present in our everyday existence, joining Earth to sky, cobweb to tree and people to each other. When we look at a web we see the thread and the woven pattern, but which part of it, physically, is connection? What we perceive as connections are actually threads that have been placed in a particular way. Connection itself does not have a separate physical presence outside of the web's shaping. Thus it is with Spirit.

The element of Spirit represents transformation. When you are ready to step onto the spiritual path of Wicca, ask Spirit to reveal a connection, a truth, a way forward. Be patient and your answer will come. Collect your own Spirit symbols and nurture your own Spirit by meditating on them often.

Spirit is the element of transformation.

WORKING WITH SPIRIT

1 Consider the complex connections in your own life. Calculate how many people you come into personal contact with in an average week. On that basis, assess the number of people each one of your connections has contact with.

2 Continue calculating outwards to further 'contact' generations. Notice how rapidly the numbers escalate into the thousands. Consider what this tells you about the impact that we have on others on a daily basis.

3 Think about the air we breathe in a similar way; also the heat we create, the water cycle, the genetic material we humans share.

Spirit is sometimes represented by crystals.

RITUAL WELCOME TO SPIRIT

Officer for Spirit:
In the centre, the element of Spirit; connection and magic, weaver and web, you are honoured in this circle. Be present at our rites and bring to this circle your gifts of transformation.

Officer lights a purple or white candle in the centre:
Hail and welcome!

All:
Hail and welcome!

VISUALIZATION

THE IMPORTANCE OF VISUALIZATION

Visualization is a crucial part of a witch's spiritual and magical tool-kit. The ability to hold in our mind's eye aspects of our inner, spiritual landscape or to imagine the intended outcome of a spell is an important part of self-development, spell-work and ritual. Visualization is used routinely to encapsulate the intent of the actions we are undertaking, and to direct the energy we are raising towards its goal. In magical and spiritual work, clarity of intention is fundamental to the success of our work and visualization is an integral part of craft discipline.

THE POWER WITHIN

This technique increases our potential to receive growth-enhancing clues from our deep intuitive selves. Going on guided journeys of discovery to our inner, spiritual and emotional landscapes is particularly important to our development as spiritual beings. This is precisely why visualization is so embedded in Wicca as a developmental tool and as a means of communication with the deities. It enhances our ability to 'envisage' routinely during circle and spell-work, certainly, but it also helps us to discover the power that we all have within ourselves.

If you were a natural 'day-dreamer' as a child, you may find it easy to slip into visualization. Those of us who are still quite adept at drifting off into a 'world of our own' are actually good natural story-tellers; we tell ourselves stories that we play out in our imaginations. But everybody has the basic ability to imagine. It simply requires a conscious effort to reclaim our imaginative faculties – particularly those who were discouraged from 'day-dreaming' at school or at home – and this will come with practice.

Some of us are more 'visual' than others and can produce vivid imagery inside our heads, while others find it easier to focus on a narrative pattern – a storyline with causes and consequences, actions and outcomes. It really doesn't matter which type of imagining you use; it is more important that you learn to focus it to steer guided inner journeys, and develop the ability to 'receive' and recognize the sometimes unexpected images and impressions that can emerge during the process.

The exploration of inner landscapes is part of visualization.

Details you encounter on your inner journeys are clues to guide you on your spiritual path.

Visualization is a form of meditation in that it deflects distracting thoughts of the everyday by providing a mental 'map' of an inner journey. While the left-hand side of the brain is occupied with the 'story' or 'map' coordinates, the right-hand side of the brain – associated with random creativity, psychic abilities and magic – is free to become a transmitter and receiver. Important messages from the deep inner self, which is connected with the Whole, with Spirit, with the God or Goddess, may emerge during inner journeys.

Some people record a journey and play it back on tape so that they can concentrate on the journey itself. Others get a friend to read it aloud or, if in a group, nominate someone to guide everyone else through the visualization. Reading out loud requires some expertise on the part of the 'reader' or guide, who needs

to be aware of the appropriate speed at which to proceed, and the length of pauses involved. Facilitating visualizations sensitively is itself an acquired skill!

Over the following pages, you will find guidance for visualizations for a variety of purposes. The best way to start is to read the visualization through at least three times, memorizing key aspects of the journey, then carry out the visualization from memory. You do not have to remember it word for word, just the main points. Keep a note pad and pen next to you so that you can record anything that strikes you as important as soon as you emerge from your inner journey. Just as we forget dreams after waking, the images, symbols and words given to us during visualizations fade like fairy gold in daylight unless we remember to write them down.

PREPARATION

When undertaking the following visualization exercises there are several things to bear in mind, particularly if you are a beginner. First, be patient with yourself; very few of us achieve spectacular results the first time we undertake a guided inner journey, and most of us drift off or lose concentration until we become more experienced. All that is needed is practice, patience and more practice! You will need a quiet place where you will be undisturbed for the duration of your journey – up to 30 minutes.

TOTAL RELAXATION

You also need to relax, concentrating on slowing your breathing, relaxing your muscles and finding a position in which you will be comfortable. Relaxed positioning is a prerequisite to any type of magical, spiritual or circle work, so it is a good idea to practise this.

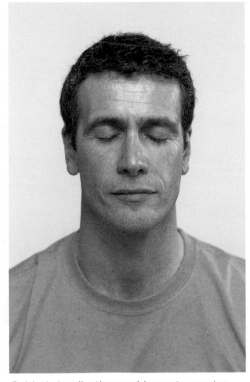

Guided visualization enables us to receive important messages from the inner self.

HOW TO PREPARE FOR VISUALIZATION

1 Start by closing your eyes. Take three deep breaths, breathing in calm and breathing out stress, anxieties and distracting thoughts.

2 The next seven breaths draw energy from the ground below you and the Earth below that, up through an imaginary column running right through the centre of your body.

3 The first breath lights up the energy point or chakra at the base of your spine, which is a red light or flower. The second lights the sacral chakra (below the belly button), which is orange. The third breath activates the solar plexus chakra which is yellow; the fourth the heart chakra which is green; the fifth the throat chakra which is blue; and the sixth the third-eye chakra (forehead) which is violet.

4 The seventh breath opens the crown chakra of pure white light. Allow it to shower over you and connect back with the Earth energy upon which you are drawing.

5 Visualize a circle of white light all around you. This creates sacred space between the everyday world and the inner world into which you are about to journey.

6 When your visualization is over and you have made notes, 'close down' the circle and the energy centres you have activated, leaving the base of spine chakra and the crown chakra open just a little. Neglecting to 'close down' can leave you over-sensitized and vulnerable to other people's negative energies.

7 Finish your visualization by eating and drinking something to 'ground' yourself as you return to the everyday world – this is important!

Visualization work can take place indoors or out in the open.

ELEMENTAL BALANCING

Given that one of the key concerns of Wicca is to restore balance to our lives and our relationship with the Earth, it is not surprising that we focus on finding that balance within ourselves. One way we do this is through our relationship with the elements Air, Fire, Water and Earth. We may find ourselves working more with one element than with others; for example, when I am writing, I feel most connected with Air. This is a natural reflection of our work with the sacred elements.

However, we may find ourselves over-dependent on one element, or have problems relating to a particular element for no apparent reason. The best way to address this is to balance the elements within us. This visualization is suited to all seekers of balance. You can use it as many times as you wish, and most covens have a version that they use as a way of 'grounding' before magical work or as a part of training.

You can see the elements at work in nature in the Sun, wind and rain.

VISUALIZATION

Prior to undertaking the preparations as detailed on pages 87–89, give yourself a thorough physical 'shake-down' to loosen joints and muscles, and physically 'brush' away your everyday stresses, anxieties and concerns.

1 When your breathing has slowed down, lie on the ground and make yourself comfortable. Close your eyes and allow your attention to sink deep into your body.

2 Imagine yourself sinking through your body, through the floor and down into the Earth below. Sink deeply into the layers of clay, chalk, rock and hollows beneath. Move deeper still, feeling the weight of all the layers of roots, plants, seeds, fungi, loam, stones and bones above you. Sink further still, until you lie within a cavern. What do you see there? What do you smell? What do you feel? Allow your own body to merge with the matter around you, until there is no distinction between your body and the Earth-body. Stay in this state for as long as you are able.

3 When you are ready, notice the moisture around you. Warm water washes the edges of your body so that you become aware of a separation between yourself and the Earth. The flow increases until you are entirely surrounded, floating in a sac of clear water. You can breathe easily as you float within it. Become aware of the flow around you and within you. Feel the blood coursing through your veins, the water of your body tissue. Allow yourself to merge with the water and let it carry you out of your Earth-womb into a sea, pulsing with currents and flows of different temperature.

4 Become one with the current and flow and the waves that break on the shore. Spend as much time as you are able merged with Water.

5 When ready, allow the current to wash you ashore on to a warm beach, where the Sun dries your skin. Take a draught of Air into your lungs and exhale fully. Take in three deep breaths and exhale as far as you can. On the next

breath, feel yourself rise above the sand and on the next, rise higher, suspended above the beach. Allow each breath to take you higher, and let your body float on the currents of Air. Imagine the breezes blowing your spirit-body along. Experiment with flight and swoop through the sky. Become aware of the oxygen pulsing through your blood, giving essential energy to your body. Rise higher and stay in flight for as long as you wish.

6 When ready, rise towards the heat and light of the Sun. Allow yourself to absorb its energy and become aware of the heat of your own body. Rise until you are absorbed into the Sun's fire, becoming completely radiant and filled with light and warmth. Merge your spirit-body with the body of the Sun, lighting the solar system with your strength. How does this feel? Remain in this state for as long as you wish or are able.

7 When ready, slowly return to your surroundings, bringing with you the energy and gifts of the elements with which you have merged. Carry that awareness with you throughout your rituals and spell-work, or when you wish to restore balance in your life. Close down according to the guidance on page 88.

SAMHAIN JOURNEY

This is the first of a set of seasonal visualizations intended to help you celebrate specific festivals. You can undertake these journeys individually or nominate a member of your group to lead you through these path-workings. You will notice that Yule and Ostara are missing; these have been appropriated to some extent by Christianity and by secular society. The challenge is to construct your own inner journeys for these festivals, in order to help you encounter an authentic 'Yule' and 'Eostre'. Read through and experience some of the visualizations offered here for ideas.

Samhain is the day of the ancestors, the time to honour our dead. We may journey to their isle and speak with them, but we may not join them on the Isle of the Dead. There are not many 'don'ts' in this book but please observe this warning – if you try to cross over to the isle, you may find your dreams disturbed, or that your psychic development becomes hampered quite seriously.

The Samhain journey takes us to the Isle of the Dead.

Before undertaking preparations as detailed on pages 87–89, ensure that you are properly 'grounded', and have a familiar object close at hand that you can physically hold when you return from your inner journey. This will help to 'anchor' you in consensual reality when the visualization has ended.

1 Close your eyes and become aware of any intrusive thoughts. Mentally 'bat' them away as you prepare to enter the inner worlds.

2 As you enter the space within, become aware of the wash of waves in the distance. Allow this sound to become louder as you draw nearer to its source. Open your inner senses – feel the drag of breezes on your skin, the taste of salt, the sensation of dry sand under your feet. Open your inner vision to see that you are on a seashore. Take note of your surroundings. What colour is the sand, the sky? Walk to the water's edge until you find a craft. Step into the boat and notice its colour, its details. Is anybody else in the boat? Do they speak to you? What do you notice as the boat moves out to sea? What do you hear?

3 When the boat lands, notice the details of its mooring place. This is a small island, joined to a vaster shore by a bridge. What does the bridge look like; what and who is on the other shore? You may hear voices or sounds that are familiar and strange, see faces you know and faces of strangers. Those who wish to speak to you will approach the far end of the bridge. You may face them from your side of the bridge, but you may not cross. If anybody wishes to speak with you, they will do so. You may speak with the dead; you are contacting that deep part of yourself that is their memory. When you have finished speaking, bid a proper farewell and thank the guardian of the bridge for your time there. Should you wish, you may ask the guardian who he or she is and what his or her purpose is. Listen carefully to the answers you receive; you may wish to

remember and note them down on your return.

4 Take a rest on your island. Think about your own life. What is your earliest memory? What have you learned during your lifetime so far? Who taught you these lessons? Are they alive or have they passed to the Summerlands? What part of them remains with you? When ready, return to the boat, and sail back to the shore from whence you came. How do you feel to leave that place? Is the journey back more difficult than the journey outwards? Is someone with you on your journey? Who is it that is travelling with you?

5 As you disembark, thank whoever travels with you and concentrate on the feeling of firm ground beneath your feet. Physically pick up the object you have chosen as your 'anchor' and slowly return to your surroundings. If you are working with others, you may wish to compare your experiences before you make notes and close down (as indicated on page 89).

6 Make sure you eat a hearty meal on your return from this journey – stamping your feet on *terra firma* is also a good antidote to any residual dreaminess!

7 Over the next month, revisit the notes you made during your visualization and see what lessons you can take from your journey to the farthest shore.

IMBOLC REAWAKENING

Imbolc witnesses the first signs of returning life after the darker days of the year. It is a time to sow seeds for new projects and renew our commitment to the principles we hold dear. This visualization helps emerge from the deep womb of winter, the darker days when our spiritual attention is turned inwards, into the light of the coming season when our attention will be turned outwards. Then we will work towards manifesting the ideas and potential we have discovered in the dark within ourselves.

This path-working acts as a catalyst to effect changes from within; at Imbolc we begin to move from concept or potential, to manifestation. Parts of this guided journey will require physical movement, so you will need to ensure adequate floor space, and some pillows or cushions to support your changing resting positions.

Imbolc is a time of emergence.

VISUALIZATION

Undertake the preparations detailed on pages 87–89.

1 On the floor, take up your normal sleeping position. When settled, close your eyes and concentrate on your heartbeat for 30 beats. Tune into this pulse as it slows, and if you cannot hear it, imagine the sound. Through the floor, try to feel another great, slow heartbeat. It matches yours. Follow that heartbeat down, deep into the spaces below the floor, through the supports and foundations of the building down into the Earth, roots, clay and chalk of the rich soil.

2 As your attention sinks deeper, hear the heartbeat below you growing louder – you may even feel it. Let your heartbeat slow to match the heartbeat of the Earth body. When these heartbeats match, allow your heartbeat to merge with that of the Earth. Concentrate on this shared heartbeat. What do you feel? Are you aware of other life within you? Do you feel sleepy or awake and alive?

3 Become aware of the seeds, bulbs, tubers and roots within the Earth body. What does the Earth offer them? What do they take from the Earth? Move your attention towards a seed. Merge with that seed and become the life within it. Physically imitate how you feel as the life within that seed. Staying in that position, think about the potential and the ideas that lie within you. How are these like and/ or unlike the life in the seed? Allow this potential, these ideas, to merge with you-as-seed.

4 Consider this carefully, then become aware of the soil around you warming up. Become aware of nourishing warmth coming down from the surface. What does this do to the life within you? Physically imitate how you think the life within the seed responds to the heat. Become aware of the light of the surface coming closer to you. Physically mimic the effect this has on the life within you, the seed. Continue the process

of the seed's response to the sunlight. Continue moving in response to how you feel as seed/potential within. When the process is complete, open your eyes. What physical position are you in? If you can, keep this position and slowly return your consciousness to human form.

5 When you have completed this change, close your eyes again and assume a comfortable standing or sitting position, whichever is closest to the position in which you find yourself.

6 What potential or ideas did you identify within yourself? Are you aware of how these came into being? What protects/shelters and nourishes these? What spurs them towards growth? What will continue to feed them when they have grown and flourished? What would prevent them from growing to maturity and producing other 'seeds'? How will you ensure that they come to manifestation and fruition?

7 When you are satisfied that you have answered these questions, relax and listen to your heartbeat, still merged with the Earth. Listen closely and feel for 30 heartbeats, then separate your heart and slowly shift your consciousness towards your physical surroundings before returning to consensual reality.

8 Close down now, in accordance with the guidelines on page 89.

9 If you carry out this exercise in a group, you may wish to compare your experiences before you note down the most significant aspects of your journey. Return to these ideas over the following spring and summer months to check that you have tended the 'seeds' of your ideas, and that your new ideas and projects have not been left behind.

BELTANE AND THE GREEN MAN

The beginning of May (end of October in the southern hemisphere) heralds the first blossom of the hawthorn tree. The greenwoods and meadows flourish and the Green Man, consort of the Goddess, puts aside the wilder part of his nature to marry her under the oak. To enter the realm of the Green Man is to encounter the wilder side of our own natures and to fully appreciate our physicality. This visualization is best undertaken outdoors, and works well for solo path-workers as well as with a group.

If you are working alone you could take along a friend to guarantee your privacy and safety. Take along a little bread and fruit juice.

The stag is a symbol of Herne, guardian of the greenwood.

VISUALIZATION

Prior to undertaking the preparations detailed on pages 87–89, find a leafy tree with a large trunk against which you can sit and lean your back while you are journeying.

1 Close your eyes and concentrate on the touch of the tree-bark against your back. Allow yourself to feel the warmth and life in the tree. Listen to any sounds coming from within it, from its branches. Focus your attention on the tree, and imagine your body taking on some of its characteristics. Which characteristics would you wish to take on, symbolically, emotionally or physically? Which would you prefer not to acquire? Why?

2 When you have answered these questions and mentally taken on those aspects of the tree that you wish to, become aware of the most desirable aspects of your own physical body. Try to identify something you like about your physical self. Now imagine that you hear someone approach. Open your inner eyes and greet the figure who stands before you. Do you recognize the figure or any aspect of him or her? Is the figure alone or accompanied? What is he or she carrying? The figure lays an object on the ground before you or offers it to you to take. They are honouring those aspects of your physical self that you have identified as attractive or especially likeable. Accept this gift – take note of what it is, as this may be important to you in future.

3 The figure invites you to follow them – allow your spirit-body to do this. How does the figure move? Do you adjust your movement to match theirs? Who or what else accompanies you? Allow the figure to lead you deep into the greenwood, taking note of all the life teeming around you. Be aware of the sensation of the forest floor on your feet, the

brush of the Sun and breeze on your body, and the scents that rise from the ground. If you see anything edible, taste it. What can you hear? What activities are taking place around you? Do you feel able to join in? Why do you?

4 Use what you find around you to decorate yourself – blossoms, feathers or trailing leaves. Be conscious of how your physical body is responding to the activities of your spirit-self.

5 Deep in the forest, you see a very old building. Go towards it and explore. What is its condition? What symbols do you find among its decorations or structure? Do they tell you anything about the realm in which you are journeying or the figure(s) you encounter there? What do they tell you about your chosen spiritual path/ yourself? When you are ready to leave, approach the figure that has led you there, and thank them for your experience.

They may speak with you – listen to what they have to say and accept anything they have to offer you.

6 Allow the scene around you to fade. Direct your attention to the tree-trunk against your back. Slowly separate from the tree, mentally allowing the physical aspects you acquired during your journey to fade. Keep within you any symbolic and emotional aspects you adopted from it; this is a gift from the greenwood. Gently return to everyday consciousness and to your surroundings.

7 After you have jotted down any notes, close down in accordance with the guidelines on page 89.

8 Finally eat the bread and drink some fruit juice, leaving a little to pour into the Earth to honour the tree that has been your guardian. Remember to leave some bread for the birds.

LITHA AND THE TURNING OF THE WHEEL

The summer solstice is the longest day of the year and many witches take to the hillsides and sacred places to greet the Litha sunrise. The visualization for this festival is intended for those staying out to witness the turning of the year's wheel. Ideally, it is a journey to be undertaken just before the sky grows light. If you are working alone, ensure that you will be secure and private. You will need a blanket or mat to sit on and a chalice or wineglass of orange juice.

Stonehenge in Wiltshire, England, is aligned with the summer solstice sunrise.

VISUALIZATION

Prior to undertaking the preparations detailed on pages 87–89, find a comfortable place to sit at a vantage point facing east, so that you can view the sunrise. Place the chalice of wine or juice on the ground in front of you.

1 Close your eyes and concentrate on the space immediately behind your eyelids. Sink into the darkness within and let your attention sink from the level of your third-eye chakra to your throat, to your heart chakra and on down until it rests at your solar plexus. Focus on this energy point in your body. Picture it as a fiery wheel, growing in brilliance until it radiates outwards from your body, lighting everything around you. Allow it to diminish slightly, retaining the image of the golden spinning wheel within.

2 Consider the function of this energy point in your body. How does this part of your body react in stressful situations, surprises or shocks? How would it feel to have this energy point in an open position all of the time?

3 Relax and become aware of the ground where you sit, the life on and beneath its surface. Sensitize yourself to the temperature of the air so that you can become aware of any changes as dawn breaks. Keeping an awareness of your solar plexus energy point, allow your attention to drop further down into the deep core of the Earth. Carry your awareness through the levels of life and death that form the layers to the centre. Drop down towards the heat and light of the Earth's core. Envisage its gases and flames emerging as sulphur, steam, geysers, lava and volcanoes. Imagine the metallic core of the planet as an inner sun, shooting flames, gases and minerals into the Earth-space around it, enriching the soil and providing energy and fuel to the upper world.

4 Now transfer that thought to your own solar plexus; picture it still as a fiery wheel, spinning at the centre of your torso. What energy does this Sun-wheel provide for your body/emotions/spirit? How does it direct or distribute energy in/from your body?

5 Experience this by drawing energy up from the Earth's core into your own solar plexus, and direct it through your solar plexus towards the circle of light with which you have surrounded yourself, allowing the energy to circle around you. What does this power feel like? Allow the energy circulating around you to be drawn back through the spinning wheel of your solar plexus and return to the Earth core below.

6 As you sense it growing lighter and the temperature rising, draw into your solar plexus the heat and light from the Sun, which, though below the horizon, is already making its presence felt. Now direct the energy you are drawing from the Earth through your spinning solar plexus to the sky, and from sky via solar plexus, to Earth. Absorb into yourself some of the light and energy you are transferring between Earth and the sky.

7 Continue until the Sun rises. Stand to greet the Sun, cupping in your hands the chalice of juice. Allow the Sun's rays to fall on the liquid, and when the Sun is fully risen, drink the liquid. The energy that you take into yourself now will carry you through the darker days to come.

8 When you write up your notes, consider the image of the wheel in relation to the dance between Earth and Sun, Sun and self. Close down according to the guidance offered on page 89.

LUGHNASADH –
WINNOWING AND GATHERING

At harvest time our thoughts turn towards the gifts and blessings we have accumulated in the past year. This is a good time to evaluate our own personal 'harvests' and consider which of these we can share with others. It is also a time for sorting out the wheat from the chaff – both literally and metaphorically speaking. Just as the stalks and hulls are separated from the nourishing grain, we can decide which are the things we wish to discard, and which to keep and value.

Harvest is a time for us to consider our blessings, and to think about what we can carry forward with us into the next cycle.

This visualization can take place indoors or outside, in a group or alone. You need a pen and paper, a short length of pure wool thread and a few stalks of corn, preferably from this year's harvest. If working outdoors, it would be ideal to have a small bonfire close by. Undertake the preparations detailed on pages 87–89.

1 Hold the stalks of corn, close your eyes and focus on the life cycle they represent – from seed to green shoot, then tall stalk with ears of corn turning from green to gold beneath the Sun, producing more seed, and so on.

2 Now think of your life since the last harvest. How have you progressed and grown? What aspects of self, projects or ideas have flourished? Have you harvested these or are they still in the process of growth? What bounty and blessings have come to you in the past year? Think in terms of wealth (having enough food, shelter, warmth), health, opportunities, things you have been able to create, things that have been given freely to you, emotional support from friends, new people who have come into your life. How would you summarize these blessings? Try to encapsulate these blessings in one word. Keep that word in your head for later.

3 Now think about things that have stayed too long in your life, are no longer needed or are simply unwelcome. These can be habits, the presence of certain conditions or people, burdens, physical objects, things you have outgrown. How would you characterize these unwanted things? Try once again to capture this 'chaff' in a single word. Remember it for later.

4 Consider what you would like to carry from this harvest into next year. Imagine these blessings as stalks of corn, tied in a sheaf, arranged in stacks and placed in a basket before you. Who would you like to share your bounty with? How might you do that? How does it feel to have the fruits of your labour and gifts laid in

front of you in this way? Think forward to next harvest – what would you like to see in that basket? What do you want to achieve in the next year? Who can help you do that and how will you ensure that you have the opportunity to accomplish all that you wish in the next turn of the wheel?

5 Become aware of a figure sitting opposite you. What does they look like? Do they carry anything with them? Do they ask you for anything? Do they give you anything? Offer this year's harvest to them and await their response. Do they accept? What message do they have for you? Thank them for any gifts or advice they have to offer and then allow them to rise, walk away and/or fade into the distance.

6 Gently return to everyday consciousness, open your eyes and, on the right-hand side of the paper, write the word that encapsulates your blessings. On the left-hand side write the word that describes those things you wish to discard. Tear the paper down

the middle, and with the wool attach the 'blessing' word to your small bunch of corn.

7 Scrunch the other word up into a ball and either throw it into the fire, or burn it outside afterwards. If you are able to retrieve its ash, mix this with some compost or bury near a plant so that it can be recycled as nourishment.

8 If you are working with a group, you may wish to exchange corn 'blessings' or keep your own. Either way, the blessings should be kept until Imbolc, then burned outside and the ashes used as compost.

9 Ensure that you close down after this path-working in accordance with the advice offered on page 89.

MODRON – ARTHUR'S JOURNEY

In the wheel of the year, the autumn equinox is positioned in the west. Our pagan ancestors believed that this was the direction of death, the route taken by the soul on its way to the Summerlands. Day and night are in perfect balance at Modron, and thereafter dark triumphs and we say a sad farewell to the Sun as it 'goes into the west'. The legend of King Arthur has particular resonance at this time of year; he is the archetypal Sun King, the consort of the Earth Goddess, borne away into the west when his time is spent.

Our ancestors believed that our souls migrated to the Summerlands to the west of the world, where the Sun sets.

VISUALIZATION

This visualization can be used as part of a Modron ritual or as preparation for it. If you are able to do this out of doors, a waterside location is ideal. You will need to stand and move around at the beginning of this meditation so ensure that you have ample space. Have a blue candle in a holder close to hand. Undertake the preparations outlined on pages 87–89 before starting.

1 Stand with eyes open facing north, the place where the Sun sits below the horizon. How do you feel when you face this direction? With what do you associate it? Turn towards the east, the place of the sunrise and dawn. How do you feel when you face this direction? With what do you associate it?

2 Turn on your heel to your right again, so that you are facing south, where the Sun is at its zenith at noon. How do you feel when you face this direction? With what do you associate it? Turn again to face full west, the direction of the sunset, of dusk. Sit down and gently close your eyes.

3 With your mind's eye, picture a seascape, with the sea gently rocking. The Sun is sinking towards the horizon, glowing orange in the sky and throwing its reflected rays across the water. It lights a clear path towards the sunset. Think about how this scene makes you feel?

4 There is a craft setting sail towards the Sun. What colour are its sails? What is in the boat? Think back to the days of summer just passed. What did that summer bring you? What did it take away? Do you have any regrets of things done or left undone; relationships that ended?

5 On the shore is a quiver of arrows and a bow next to a small fire. Each arrow represents the things that summer has brought and taken away again. Mentally name each arrow with something the summer brought as you pick them up and fix them to the bow. Dip each tip into the fire. Take aim and shoot the flaming arrows over the water into the sails and hull of the departing boat. Continue until you have fired all arrows.

6 Raise your right hand in farewell to the boat and everything that you have sent with it; watch it sail away until you can no longer see it. When it has disappeared, the rim of the Sun will sink below the horizon in the distance.

7 Allow this vision to fade and gradually return to your surroundings. Before you make any notes or close down, consider all the gifts of summer, both personal and communal. Think about the Sun's warmth and how it warmed and ripened the crops and fruits. Remember how it enabled people to get together outdoors, to carry out pursuits closed to them in winter. Think about good times you shared with friends and/or family during the warm season. Give thanks to the Sun and light your blue candle in memory of summer's happy days.

8 When you make notes, ask yourself what you associate with the west and how the Sun's demise affects you emotionally, physically or spiritually. Close down in accordance with the guidance offered on page 89.

THE TEMPLE OF THE MOON

In the mystical Qabalah, the sphere of the Moon is called 'Yesod' and is associated with the unconscious mind, with cycles of existence and with psychic and magical abilities. This ties in with the symbolism and experiences that witches associate with the Moon, and is a good starting point for those who wish to discover more about their spiritual direction. The following visualization is a favourite in more traditional covens where newcomers are 'trained' by a high priest or priestess.

This inner journey helps new Wiccans move beyond the realm of the rational and into what I call 'Goddess-space'. This is the chaotic place-time of possibility and potential, the foundation of all creation and magic, which those who seek a magical life must experience. We need to be in touch with Moon energy to grow spiritually and extend our powers magically. This is a potent visualization, so it is advisable to leave at least three lunar cycle between visits.

The Moon is the ruler of dreams.

VISUALIZATION

Undertake preparations as detailed on pages 87–89.

1 Close your eyes and concentrate on breathing in through your nose and out through your mouth, thinking only of your breathing.

2 When fully relaxed, allow your attention to sink deep into yourself, dropping from the head to the throat chakra, then to the heart and further down to your solar plexus. Allow your attention to sink further until you come to rest at your centre.

3 Imagine yourself on a dark beach with only the light of the stars to pick out the details of your surroundings. Walk towards the waves breaking on the sand and into the water. How does the water feel? Is it cold and refreshing or warm and embracing?

4 Walk into the deep water until the waves cover your head and you are walking on the seabed. You can breathe and move quite easily in this environment. Walk until the seabed ascends and you emerge from the waves on another shore. Walk forwards onto the beach. The Moon has risen; note its phase.

5 Walk along the shore until you come to a path through the greenery that surrounds the beach. What kind of trees and plants are found here?

6 Follow the path leading towards a white marble building. Note its shape. Move towards the door, taking note of its features, and open it. Enter the building; the door will close behind you. Move to the centre of the space, where moonlight pours down. Is the building roofed or open to the elements? In the surrounding walls are many curtains, hiding doorways. Choose one to go through.

7 Draw its curtain aside, noting the colour and any symbols, and push open the door. This may lead into an open space or another building. Pass through the door into the realm you have chosen.

8 A figure either waits for you or will approach you. Allow them to speak first – they have a gift from the temple of the Moon for you. Accept it with thanks. Spend some time inspecting the object. Hold it to your chest and allow it to merge into your spirit-body through your solar plexus. Allow its essence to ascend, with your attention, from solar plexus to heart, from heart to throat, and from throat to your third-eye chakra.

9 When ready, slowly return to everyday consciousness and make notes of all that has passed during your journey. Close down in accordance with the guidance on pages 89.

The object you have been given may appear in your dreams, which should be more vivid following this path-working. Meditate on the Moon card in the Tarot – what does the Moon teach those who are on the Wiccan path? Spend time connecting with the lunar cycle, noting its impact on your dreams and psychic abilities, noting changes in your energy levels throughout the month. Most importantly, see if you can discover what your 'gift' represents in terms of your magical skills.

THE
SACRED CIRCLE

THE SACRED CIRCLE

The circle represents a universal and spiritually relevant paradox – a shape without beginning and without end. It visually describes eternity, the mysterious cycles of existence and the often uncanny circularity of our own lives. Our ancient ancestors recognized the sacred significance of this shape and laid out many of their monuments in circle-form. Around Europe, for example, are the scattered remains of wooden and stone circles, aligned with specific stellar or solar rises and settings, many of which contain inner circles.

The circle symbolizes the miraculous cycle of existence.

Many commentators have noted the yonic symbolism attached to such formations – that the circle represents that sacred place in the body from which women push life into the world. The fact that there are circles within circles seems to confirm the mystical association between the physical act of giving birth and the mystery of regeneration.

SETTING BOUNDARIES

In Wicca, we do most of our ritual and spell-work within a circle, cast by a witch in order to define the boundaries of the place where we come face to face with our deities, where we work magic and enter altered states of consciousness. This space is sacred because it is dedicated to the God and Goddess and their work. It also contains what we call the 'space between the

Our ancestors left clues to their spiritual beliefs on the landscape.

worlds', a place that is neither wholly set in the everyday nor wholly in the realm of Spirit, but marked out and set aside for the wise who can travel between these worlds and bring back wisdom. The space is dedicated to the god or goddess within us, as well as the God and Goddess of the rest of the existence. Every time we step into the circle, we are honouring the divine within ourselves and growing and developing our sacred potential in the company of the deity.

SACRED SPACE

The boundaries of the circle are protected by the elements and the deities we call in and honour. This is not to protect us from B-movie type monsters or demons that we may inadvertently 'raise' or attract through our work – it doesn't work like that! The circle protects us from the crowding distraction of everyday concerns, so that we can stand back from the minutiae of our busy lives. It allows us to temporarily set aside the mantle of our daily roles. The boundaries we set allow us to claim the space as specific to a sacred purpose, as special.

The line of the circle is a boundary – it allows us to contain the power we raise within it and holds it until we are ready to release it into the wider world to do its work. In this respect, it is a little like a pot with a lid, in which we are boiling a good soup – we wouldn't place the ingredients on the plate before they were properly cooked, so we keep the lid on the pan until it is ready. It is exactly the same with magic and ritual work – the ingredients of the spell or ritual need to be properly energized and blended before they are ready to emerge as a power and energy in the wider web of existence.

SPACE BETWEEN WORLDS

An important point to note is that the sacred circle is not a flat, two-dimensional shape; it is actually a sphere that encompasses the whole sacred space. It extends above and below the human participants, intersecting floors and ceilings and often walls. It is a world both within and outside of the world of our everyday existence or consensual reality; it allows us to step outside of that reality and into another – while at the same time remaining connected with our 'baseline' everyday existence. Circle-space is also a part of the world of Spirit, the place of connection, interconnection, formation and transformation. This is another paradox of the circle; it offers a space between the worlds, but

incorporates aspects of those worlds at the same times as it provides a space apart from them.

Just as the spherical nature of the sacred space provides us with a perfected and whole 'circle', a reflection of itself above and below the line of the ground on which

These ancient spiral carvings on stone can be found in Newgrange Mound, Ireland.

we physically work, so the worlds between which we work are reflected within that space. As we say in Wicca: 'As above: So below'. The nature of the circle makes it possible for us to symbolize, represent and encapsulate aspects of our daily world, and enact symbolic changes that we wish to actualize within consensual reality.

We use the symbolic as a doorway through which we can touch and then draw through threads from the world of Spirit, which we then weave into a new pattern. This is how magic works – by accessing the worlds between which we move and bringing them together. Ironically, in order to do this, we first have to

move outside of both worlds; and this can only be done from within the sacred space of the circle.

EVER-CHANGING

Another shape closely associated with the circle is the spiral – a progressive circle that if seen three-dimensionally might closely resemble an elongated spring. Some Wiccans acknowledge the close links between the spiral and the circle because we see the circle as a symbol of constant change and progression. Nothing in the Universe stays the same and this is true of the circle. For us, just as all gods and goddesses are one God and Goddess but not all gods

and goddesses are the same, all circles are the one great circle of being, but every circle is different. We do not ever come out of the circle exactly the same person who goes in; it is like the saying that one can never cross the same river twice. By definition, the river changes because time passes, and the same is true of the circle. Within this progression of changes, the circle can be seen as a simple expression of the spiral – symbol of the eternal flux of all time-space-matter.

There is an additional and important reason why each circle is different; it is the space of transformation. If the circle is different each time, it is also true that whatever we take with

The spiral expresses the eternal journey of time-space-matter.

us becomes altered in some way as a result of stepping into it. Some witches notice early on that there is a sort of 'magnifying' effect at work within sacred space; this is a natural consequence of the intensity of what we experience there, and ensues from close contact with the realm of Spirit. What we carry with us to the circle grows in our consciousness to the point where we can see it properly, occasionally becoming so big that we have to deal with it. This can be anything from a strength that we are failing to recognize and develop, to a bad habit that needs to be dealt with.

What we deal out to others within the circle, as in life, is what is returned to us; it is what we become. In the circle, this effect is amplified manifold.

TIME LAPSE

You may notice when you begin circle-work that there is a slight discrepancy in time perception between the world of consensual reality and the space between the two worlds. Many witches notice that, occasionally, what seems to be no more than an hour in the circle is three hours or more outside of it. The most common experience seems to be the rapidity with which time passes in circle-space. It is not unknown, however, for the reverse to be experienced, especially when deep meditation work is being undertaken. On such occasions, celebrants may leave the circle feeling as though they have been away for hours, and find that only 45 minutes has passed. In tales of the Celtic Otherworld, human visitors to the world of Faery invariably experience a sense of time-disorientation; what passes for a day in the realm of Faery is found to be a year in the mortal realm, and seven years becomes seven hundred. It is tempting to speculate on the origins of these peculiar time-lapses, and whether the tales have absorbed aspects of tribal shamanic practice, where those who walk between the worlds experience time-changes.

UNIVERSAL ENERGY

The shape of the circle also describes the progression of our planet around the Sun. The circle is always cast in a *deosil* (pronounced day-sill) or 'sunwise' – clockwise direction. Traditionally, when building magical and ritual energy, celebrants try to ensure that they move deosil while in the circle to ensure that they keep the energy moving in the right direction. Sometimes participants will even move in a *widdershins* or anti-sunwise – anti-clockwise direction, when a banishing ritual is being enacted. When you become familiar with the energies that you yourself work with as a witch, then you will be able to decide what works best once you are within sacred space. However, the circle is almost universally cast deosil in Wicca.

ALTARS AND SACRED SPACES

The classic definition of an altar is a place upon which sacrifices or gifts are offered to deities; if a physical description accompanies this definition, it suggests that an altar is a 'raised' structure or a 'high place'. Although this is a narrow idea of what an altar is, it does convey the notion that it holds things that are sacred and special, and may be a space in which gifts or offerings are left. In Wicca, our deities do not demand sacrifice. However, we do use altars in Wicca for several functions.

ALTAR FORMS

Altars come in many shapes and forms. They can be as simple as a flat rock placed in a shaded corner of a garden or woodland or as elaborate as an indoor permanent table decorated with embroidered cloths, canopied and covered in candles, herbs, flowers and statues or other sacred imagery.

An altar might be temporary – for example, a cloth-covered chest set up for the duration of a circle and then dismantled or a tree stump that you surround with a ring of stones and twigs only when you perform circle work. But an altar can also be permanent – a corner shelf in an apartment or a marble table on a hillside. What really matters is the intent with which an altar is established. Its sacred purpose is what makes it an altar.

Incense is often burned in order to consecrate a sacred space.

Altars provide a focus for spell-work and spiritual development.

SACRED CIRCLE ALTARS

An altar provides a focal point for sacred and magical activity within the circle. Traditionally set up in the north, but sometimes placed at the centre, the place of Spirit, the altar holds the tools and ingredients of ritual and may hold wands, athames (witches' knives), chalices, pentacles (see pages 126–127) and bowls of salt and water, herbs, candles, crystals, mortar and pestle, or depictions of the deities. The altar also provides a practical working surface upon which to carry out the necessary activities when performing a spell or ritual – mixing herbs, anointing candles, 'exorcising' water and blessing salt (see pages 126–127). The ingredients for spells, once carried out, sometimes rest here until the end of the circle. When tools, spells or items need blessing or consecrating for a sacred purpose, they are brought to the altar – a place where things are made sacred, not just a place where sacred things are housed.

Altars can be placed indoors or out.

OUTSIDE ALTARS

Outside of the circle, altars serve many different purposes. In my garden, the big flat stone surrounded by many other rounder stones, planted around with rock roses and rosemary, is an altar to the Goddess. I have to sit on the ground to work on it, which brings me physically down to Earth. I use it as a focal point when I want to talk to the Goddess or a particular goddess, and I can burn incense and leave flowers or stones on it as offerings to her. In my home, the mantelpiece above the main hearth is an altar which variously houses offerings to particular goddesses, the physical ingredients for ongoing spell-work, candles and little offerings – feathers, flowers, cards, which honour the Goddess within. I have friends who have built altars that resemble shrines, out of stones and rocks and woven copper wire – these are focal points for meditation and visual journeys, spell-work, gifts to the Goddess, and a place to light candles to remember the dead.

In the open there are often natural 'altars', especially at ancient sites; these may be rocks where people leave coins, feathers, herbs or seeds for the birds and animals that frequent the place, or even a space on the ground below an old tree, or before a sacred well or spring. Sometimes trees near such places are dressed with 'clouties' – ribbons or strips of material that contain wishes or are simply devotional offerings to the deities of that place. If you do build an altar or leave devotional offerings at an outdoor space, it is particularly important that you use biodegradable materials so that, in time, they return to nature without polluting the environment.

Building an altar in your home is relatively simple – decide its purpose, find a suitable location and gather to it those items that you feel will best serve its function. Choose appropriate symbols, colours and items for it through meditation, intuition and research. Once you have built your own altar, whether it is a corner shelf with a tea-light and a few shells and stones, or an elaborate shrine hung with embroidered cloths, treat it with the respect that it, you and the God and Goddess deserve.

Salt and water are used to cleanse indoor space in preparation for a ritual.

CIRCLE WORK

The space in which a circle is cast is customarily cleared of both physical and psychic detritus. If indoors, the space is traditionally 'cleansed' by scattering specially prepared salt water all around it. The water is first 'exorcised'; this requires you to relax, draw in energy from the Earth through your energy points (chakras) and direct it through your hand to the water to drive out all surplus energies it may have absorbed.

The form of words can range from the traditional: 'I exorcise thee O creature of water that thou cast out from thee all uncleanlinesses and impurities'; to the more basic: 'I cleanse you, water, in the name of the Goddess'.

The same hand is used to bless the salt, a natural purifier, saying: 'Blessings upon this creature of salt, may all malignancy be cast hence from that all good enter herein'; or 'The blessings of the Goddess be upon this salt'. It is then poured into the water, stirred together either with a few words: 'May this salt water serve to purify this space and bless my art'. Sometime no words are spoken at all.

The salt water is scattered around the room deosil, starting in the east, then sprinkled over the participants. It is then time to cast the circle (see pages 130–131). In the open, however, salt and water should not be used as this will kill plant life where it is scattered, and open space in a natural setting does not need cleansing or purifying in the same way as indoor space which is also used for other purposes.

SETTING THE ELEMENTS

Prior to cleansing the space, you should set up the 'quarters' – the directions for the sacred elements. Candles, cloths and symbols for Air, Fire, Water and Earth are placed around the circle in the cardinal directions east, south, west and north respectively. Corresponding colours for each are: yellow for Air, red for Fire, blue for Water, and green for Earth. In the centre, a purple or white candle represents Spirit. If you find it difficult to obtain coloured candles, tea-lights work just as well. Some circles decorate the quarters with

Coven chalices contain wine or juice to be shared in the circle.

Wands and athames are associated with Air and Fire, pentacles with Earth.

symbols relevant to the appropriate element – a feather for Air, a lamp for Fire, a seashell for Water and a pebble for Earth.

There are magical tools associated with circle-work. Some witches like to use an athame to do the salt and water blessing and to cast the circle, for example. This is a special knife, usually with a black handle, that has been consecrated for use in circle-work. An athame is usually blessed by dipping the blade in Water, showing it to Fire, plunging it through Air and then into Earth before being consecrated in the circle. An athame is generally used only by its owner – though some witches allow others to use theirs in circle-work. Depending

on the specific Wicca tradition within which you work, an athame is associated either with Fire or Air.

THE CHALICE AND PENTACLE

The chalice is associated with Water and is traditionally given to a witch, as it represents the element of love. This contains the wine or juice that is passed around the circle before the end of a ritual and can be used in spell work (see pages 144–163). The wine is blessed, sipped, then passed deosil, with a kiss, with the words: 'May you never thirst' or 'Blessed Be'. Some witches use a pentacle – a five-pointed star within a circle – to represent Earth. This usually takes the form of a wooden, stone or metal platter, upon which we place the bread that is passed around the circle directly after the chalice. A little is broken off and eaten, then the loaf is passed on with a kiss and with the words: 'May you never hunger' or 'Blessed Be'.

In most circles the wand is associated with Air, though in some traditions this symbolism is reversed with that of Fire. A wand can be used in much the same way as an athame – to direct energy. Wands take many forms; they are usually wooden but may sometimes be made from quartz or copper. Their designs vary from very simple polished wood to extremely elaborate, set with semi-precious stones and carved with magical symbols.

In circles that have an initiatory tradition, the cords are placed at the centre. These are the shroud 'measures' (circumference of head, around the heart and the exact height) of a witch and are magically linked with them. They are placed in the centre of the circle as they are seen as the umbilical that links us to the realm of Spirit.

On a final note, traditionally, once a circle is cast, no one leaves it until it is dispersed, with the exception of an emergency. This is to retain the integrity of the sacred space within the cast circle.

Circle-work with others can be inspiring and uplifting.

HOW TO CAST A CIRCLE

Once the space is prepared (see pages 126–127), a circle can be cast. This involves opening up your energy points or chakras, in order to make yourself the conduit for the energy needed to cast a circle. The process by which you prepare yourself is identical to that offered as a guide to preparation for visualization on pages 87–89.

PREPARING YOURSELF

Start by finding a comfortable position in which you can relax fully. Take a few slow, deep breaths. Follow steps 1 to 5 of How to Prepare for Visualization on page 88. Visualize a circle of white light around you.

When you are fully prepared, and the flow of energy has been established, concentrate on directing some of that energy via your solar plexus down through your arms and out through your athame, wand or finger. Use that energy to draw a line in the air around your ritual space. It is easier to hold the visualized circle in the mind's eye if you start this process by visualizing a circle within the room in which you are working. As your confidence grows you can move on to casting circles that encompass the whole of the room in which you are working, transcending the visible boundaries of the walls, ceiling and floor.

Lighting the candles marks the final preparatory step prior to casting a circle.

Traditionally, one nods to the north and begins casting in the east, extending the arms to direct the energy outwards and moving deosil. This is known as 'describing' a circle. As you return to the starting point, seal it with a few words, for example: 'I cast this circle as a boundary between the worlds; a container of the power I/we raise and a guardian and protector of all who stand within.'

Welcome in the elements, beginning in the east and moving deosil. Use your own form of welcome or, as a working guide, it is usual to name the qualities each element brings to the circle before lighting the appropriate candle in its honour: 'In the east, the element of Air, bringing to this circle the gifts of clarity and communication, you are honoured in this circle. Hail and welcome.' It is usual, if working with a group, for all participants to repeat the last phrase.

CLOSING A CIRCLE

At the end of a ritual, thank the elements for their presence, saying: 'Hail and farewell', and extinguish the candles, though traditionally the Spirit candle is kept alight until the last person leaves saying: 'Hail and abide'. The circle is then closed by the person who cast it, either by dispersing it outwards into the Universe or drawing its energy back through the athame, finger or wand, to the body and into the Earth.

Traditionally, the circle is cast with an athame.

RITUALS AND SPELL-WORK

Although all spells are rituals, not all rituals are spells. Put simply, a ritual is an act that symbolizes or enacts something in token and is used to celebrate, commemorate or transform the object or event in question according to the will of the person(s) who carry it out. All of us have our own little everyday rituals – lighting the candles on a birthday cake, signing leaving cards for colleagues, throwing confetti or rice at weddings, wearing our own favourite scarves or shirts to sporting events or even touching wood for 'luck'.

When ritual takes place within the circle – within sacred space – it becomes especially charged with our intent, both because we raise energy and concentrate it within the circle before we release it into the web of existence, and because we conduct rituals with our deities as witnesses.

RITUALS

All spells, acts undertaken in token in order to produce change in consensual reality, are actually rituals. It is true to say that all rituals are 'magical' in their own way, but this does not make them spells. Some rituals are forms of celebration used to mark change rather than precipitate it; for example, Esbats or Moon circles which celebrate a particular phase of the Moon. We may carry out magical work and spells within it and, by participating, transform ourselves, but the ritual itself may still be primarily a marker. Some rituals celebrate, commemorate or initiate change, such as initiations, handfasting, namings or Sabbats or may be a mixture and encompass all three functions.

SPELLS

Spells, on the other hand, are rituals focused on a single intent and

Spells are part of our spiritual practice.

A ritual symbolizes or enacts the will of the witch in token.

outcome. It is common for a circle to be cast just for the purpose of performing a single spell, then closed once it is completed. This tends to happen more often in solo work, though it is not unusual for a group to get together for a single, urgent spell. As a rule, it is not wise to perform more than three spells in the course of one circle, as spells take a good deal of energy and concentration (see pages 148–149)

and humans tend to function best at a magical and psychological level in triplicities – as evidenced by the incidents of three that crop up in many stories and fairy tales.

Rituals and spells undertaken in the spirit of honesty, compassion and a genuine desire for growth and knowledge are never wasted – and in Wicca they are seen as an integral part of our spiritual practice.

TIMING OF SPELLS AND RITUALS

When you come to practise spells and conduct rituals, you will learn that there are a number of conventions within Wicca based on what we call 'correspondences'. Working with correspondences means matching the nature of the work you are undertaking with the appropriate symbols, colours, deities, day of the week, phase of the moon or planetary hour. Wicca takes an approach to magic and ritual based on principles of 'sympathy' – representing like with like – known as 'sympathetic magic'.

In the bad old days where magicians and witches divided approaches to magic into 'high' magic and 'low' magic, this approach was classed within the 'low' category. However, this was an unfortunate and misleading way of describing a highly developed tradition of tapping into deep-seated inner knowledge and power through systems of affinity symbols. This tradition has well-rooted historical precedents and is the foundation of much of what was once classed, similarly inaccurately, as 'high' magic – that which depends more heavily on its ceremonial and arcane aspects than its connection with natural knowledge.

SYMPATHETIC MAGIC

Within this sympathetic approach, timing is an important part of planning and carrying out ritual and spell-work. In Wicca, we work with the phases of the Moon partly because of the changes in energy that occur in its cycle around the Earth and partly because of the doctrine of 'sympathy'. This latter aspect sees the different phases chiefly as symbolic and so spells for increase, attraction and growth are generally cast on the waxing or growing cycle of the Moon, while spells for decrease, binding or banishing are cast on the waning or shrinking cycle of the Moon.

In the northern hemisphere the waxing phase sees the crescent growing from a right-hand arc to a full disc, while the waning phase sees the full disc shrinking on the right-hand side to an arc on the left. When the Moon is entirely covered by Earth's shadow, it is said to be a 'New' or 'Dark' Moon. This phase is particularly good for beginning new projects and enhancing psychic protection. Rituals that mark a specific occasion or celebration are

Spells cast on a waning Moon are for depletion, banishing and repelling.

best performed on a Full Moon. The phases of the Sun are also relevant in Wicca, mainly through its seasonal festivals. These are celebrated either on the day of the appropriate solstice or equinox, or in the case of the Celtic fire festivals, on the calendar date or the nearest Full Moon that follows the key events that mark it.

The days of the week have planetary correspondences as well as associated deities. This makes certain days particularly suitable for specific spells. Monday is associated with the Moon, for example, and is seen as particularly good for fertility, material growth and dream-work. It is also associated with lunar deities, and

they bring their own particular flavour to ritual or spell-work, according to which you choose. There are also astrological correspondences – for example, characteristics of certain signs that work well with particular elements in spells or rituals. Less frequently used are the planetary hours – each hour in the day is said to be ruled by a planetary influence, and some magicians time their spells almost to the minute by drawing in correspondences of Moon phase, the astrological sign of that Moon at a given time, and the appropriate planetary hour.

THE DRAW OF THE MOON

Most witches give primary importance to the Moon phase to guide them in their work for several reasons. The nature of Wiccan spirituality is such that our affinity to nature, with its changing cyclical energies, draws us to the Moon, our nearest celestial neighbour. We feel her in our tides, our biological cycles and in our dreams – at all levels, in fact. But there are historical and cultural reasons why witches favour the Moon phase above all other considerations in spiritual and magical work; for a long time primacy has been given to logos, the rational, left-brain functions. Witches envisage this changing to incorporate, as we do in our spiritual practices, elements of reflection, intuition, process and change – all of which we tend to

Astrological correspondences allow us to take into account particular influences.

Witches generally place the Moon phase above other considerations – except in urgent need.

associate with the Moon. This is not to say that we consider the Sun unimportant; simply that the Moon carries a particular significance for us.

Witches are also prepared, when need outweighs the principle of timing, to forego tradition. The guiding principle, as ever, is to 'Harm None' and if in order to stop or prevent harm we need to act quickly, then need, rather than convention and tradition, will direct our decisions on such occasions.

CORRESPONDENCES

THE FIVE ELEMENTS TABLE

The table below is a working guide to commonly recognized correspondences.

	Air	Fire	Water	Earth	Spirit
Spells	Communication, swiftness, exams, legal, knowledge and learning, conveyancing, travel	Defence, willpower, courage, inspiration	Love, healing, dream-work, women's cycles, childbirth, emotional issues	Manifestation, material wealth, shelter, fertility, growth	Initiation, transition, transformation, spiritual growth and knowledge
Herbs and plants	Lavender, eucalyptus, comfrey, wormwood, lilac	Rosemary, rue, dandelion, saffron, nettles, St John's wort	Poppy, rose, myrtle, violet, valerian, lovage, chamomile, geranium, hyacinth	Patchouli, sage, mandrake, woodbine, horehound, pennyroyal	Gentian, lotus, belladonna*, henbane* (*poisonous)
Trees	Birch, ash	Oak, rowan	Willow, apple	Cypress, pine	Elder, yew
Incenses and oils	Benzoin, sandalwood, lavender	Cinnamon, frankincense, vanilla, juniper	Myrrh, rose, absolute, orris root	Patchouli, pine resin, white sage, mandrake root	Nag champa, copal, dittany or Crete
Astrological sign	Aquarius, Gemini, Libra	Aries, Leo, Sagittarius	Pisces, Cancer, Scorpio	Taurus, Virgo, Capricorn	
Day of the week	Wednesday	Tuesday, Thursday	Monday, Friday	Saturday	Sunday
Planet(s)	Mercury	Sun, Mars	Moon, Venus, Neptune	Gaia, Saturn, Pluto	Uranus

	Air	Fire	Water	Earth	Spirit
Metal	Mercury (quicksilver)	Tin	Silver/copper	Iron/lead	Gold
Colour	White	Red	Blue	Green	Purple/white
Symbol	Upward pointing triangle traversed, feather, incense	Upward pointing triangle, flame, blade, salamanders	Downward pointing triangle, cauldron, glass, mirror	Upward pointing triangle traversed, pentacle, wood, metal, stone, crystals, dragon	Upward pointing triangle, termintated, clear quartz, web, thread
Magical Tool	Wand	Athame	Chalice	Pentacle	Cords
Animal Totems	All birds	Salamander, big cats	Fish, water-based animals	Hare, wolf, bear, serpent	Spider
Body Parts	Lungs, head	Heart	Womb, liver, kidneys, bladder	Bowels, spine	
Direction	East	South	West	North	Centre

PLANETARY HOURS

The table below is based on hourly time divisions between sunset and sunrise. This may differ in your locality according to the time of year, so in order to pinpoint the 'hour' dedicated to the appropriate planet for a spell or ritual, calculate the number of minutes between sunset and sunrise, divide by 12 and number each unit 1 to 12. The planetary 'hour' that corresponds to your needs indicates what time you need to conduct your work.

Note that the following column is a rough guide – more comprehensive systems have a rolling matrix that differs according to the days of the week. For simplicity's sake, however, the following offers an outline based on numerological and planetary correspondence.

PLANETARY HOURS TABLE

Planet	Hour
Sun	1
Moon	2
Mercury	3
Jupiter	4
Mars	5
Venus	6
Neptune	7
Pluto	8
Mercury	9
Jupiter	10
Uranus	11
Earth	12

Sample calculation

For example, you wish to cast a spell to help a friend who is having trouble concentrating on her studies.

- The best planet to work with is Mercury.

- Your local times are sunset 9.30pm, sunrise 4.30am.

  The number of minutes between sunset and sunrise is 420, divided by 12 = 35 minutes.

- The first division of time after sunset ruled by Mercury is the third 'hour':

3 x 35 minutes = 105 minutes,

9.30 pm + 105 minutes = 11.15 pm.

MOON SIGNS

It is now possible to download from the internet, a reliable ephemeris –that is, a table of predictions of planetary movements. You will also find such a table in the appendices of good astrological guides. The table will indicate at what time the Moon moves through different astrological signs. You will need to consult an ephemeris if you decide to work with the traditional correspondences outlined below. These indicate the best Moon-signs for different types of spell and are intended as an indicative guide, which you can add to as you progress in the Craft.

MOON SIGNS TABLE

Type of Spell	Aries	Taurus	Gemini	Cancer	Leo	Virgo	Libra	Scorpio	Sagittarius	Capricorn	Aquarius	Pisces
Love/ relationships			*	*			*				*	*
Healing/ emotions			*	*			*	*			*	*
Wealth/ increase		*			*	*			*	*		
Employment/ commerce			*		*				*	*	*	
Banishing/ binding	*			*		*		*				
Protection	*	*			*				*			
Fertility	*	*				*		*		*		*

DAYS OF THE WEEK

The following table, based on traditional Wiccan correspondences, can be extended as your studies in the craft develop.

	Monday	Tuesday	Wednesday	Thursday
Planet	Moon	Mars	Mercury	Jupiter
Colours	Silver, pewter, white, grey	Red	Yellow	Purple, dark blue
Deity	Selene, Nephthys, Artemis, Isis	Mars/Ares, Tiew, Oya, Kali	Mercury/Hermes, Athene, Sarasvarti, Woden	Thor, Jove/Jupiter, Rhiannon, Juno, Laxmi
Associations	Fertility, increase, dream-work	Defence, protection, inspiration, defeating obstacles, courage, sex, dance	Communication, learning, study, exams and tests, legal issues, travel, ideas, memory, science	Generosity, natural justice, expansion, property, wills, family matters
Metal	Silver	Iron	Mercury	Tin
Symbolic object	Cauldron	Arrow	Staff	Drum

	Friday	Saturday	Sunday
Planet	Venus	Saturn	Sun
Colours	Green	Black or brown	Gold
Deity	Venus/ Aphrodite, Angus, Parvarti	Hecate, Nemesis, Saturn	Brighid, Apollo, Lugh, Belissama
Associations	Love, affection, friendships, partnerships, allurement, sexuality, beauty, art	Boundaries, binding, exorcism, discipline, reduction, protection, deflection	Health, happiness, contentment, poetry
Metal	Copper	Lead	Gold
Symbolic object	Rose, star symbol	Chain, cords	Disc

SPELL-WORK
AND RITUALS

HOW MAGIC WORKS

Working with magic will give you a clearer understanding of the Craft than reading about it in a book. I have been casting spells for decades and experience has deepened my feel for magic. Sometimes I can sense intuitively whether a spell has 'taken' while I am casting it, and, on occasion, some time after I will see the individual threads coming together in everyday events.

Many witches believe that the whole of existence is connected together. This connection is visualized as a many-dimensional web, the threads of which form part of the mystery of the element of Spirit, which is the connecting force. The best way to understand this is to imagine Spirit as the connecting feature of a web – the node where different threads are held together in a pattern. The thread is the physical part of the web, but it would not be a web at all were it not for the way in which the threads are woven together. Although the thread is palpable and can be physically experienced whether or not it is part of a web, a connection – the part that is so essentially Spirit – cannot. This does not make it less real; indeed, it can be said to be the defining aspect of the web. This is how we see magic.

To cast a spell within this worldview is to weave a new pattern into the web. When we work ritual, we are working with nature, weaving into the flow a pattern, which further along will produce change. Many of us call ourselves 'patterners', which makes it easier to understand how we approach such things as spell-casting and divination. We 'tap into' the web in order to effect change by using symbols to send signals to our deeper selves – the self that is most knowledgeable and acquainted with Spirit and the God or Goddess. We work in the circle, the sacred space between the worlds, to draw in threads from the great web and work them according to our will before sending them back out into the ether with another pattern in the mix.

PREPARATION

When we go into the circle to work magic we need to prepare ourselves. This involves leaving aside the distractions of everyday worries that have a call on our attention. It does not require us to leave behind

A group focuses on a spell in preparation.

all our workaday worries; simply that we ensure that they are not distracting us from the task in hand. This is why a group spends time in preparation before circle-work, shedding the masks and burdens we wear and carry in the outside world, and activating our energy points. We prepare to change our state of consciousness in order to walk between the worlds, weave our patterns and send them out onto the great web. We need to change ourselves before we can change anything in the world around us,

and the more we do this, the more we can enter this state at will.

As you become more adept at working magic – casting spells and performing various rituals – you will recognize the different levels of energy in the circle and the ways in which they alter during the course of a ritual. Changes wrought by magical acts, when manifested, play their own part in changing consciousness, and so the cycle of change continues; you will come to identify this as you grow in experience.

PRINCIPLES, LAWS AND ETHICS

In magic there is a principle known as the Law of Threefold Return. This belief says that whatever you send out is returned to you threefold. In fact, this is just a poetic way of saying that your actions will return to you – for good or bad, and that you need to think before you act. It is a common-sense way of alerting people to the consequences of their actions and reminding them to pause before deciding what is really needed. It is both a spiritual truth and an ethical guideline.

A number of 'laws' exist, each of which claims to be the 'definitive' three, seven or nine law of magic. Firstly they are not definitive, secondly, some of them are nonsense, and thirdly, the most sensible of them amount to the same thing: Harm None. You cannot change the will of another by magic and neither should you try. The only will you can work on is your own.

Witches tend to listen and ask questions of the person seeking magical help, then they ask questions of themselves, before acting. We listen and ask in order to establish exactly what is needed. A person asking us to curse their cruel boss will be advised to approach their union for practical and legal help, and be offered healing work to help deal with the effect that bullying is having on them. We ask ourselves whether what we are asking for through magic is strictly needful – this isn't such a bad guideline to work within.

RAISING ENERGY FOR SPELL-WORK

There are a number of ways in which to raise energy during spell-work, depending on whether one works alone or with others, one's mobility, the type of spell or simply the preferences of the person putting the spell together. The energy you put into a spell actually begins in the planning stages, at the very start when you are questioning the supplicant – or yourself – to find out what is really needed. There is also the energy of the concentration we lend to a spell while we are gathering and preparing ingredients, and during the course of the spell as we imbue a symbol with our intent by our focused attention.

However, there are specific activities employed expressly within circle-work to raise the energy in order to send a spell out into the ether.

The physical means by which we work to raise energy include chanting and voice-work, anointing, drumming and dancing. The theory behind the physical means of raising energy is very simple – all existence in the Universe can be expressed as energy and movement produces and releases energy. Kinetic means of raising and releasing energy in a magically controlled environment serves to empower the spell and to propel it outwards onto the web. Within groups, dancing and chanting serve to bond people to the purpose of the spell-work and act as a way of blending the energies of the participants. It opens the doorway to the deeper self, so that we can communicate outside of spoken or written language and move beyond the symbolic. This provides us with the means to move into an altered state, which better enables us to walk between the worlds.

Raising energy to empower a spell is basic to all spellwork.

DIRECTING AND RELEASING ENERGY

Directing and releasing energy takes place at various points in circle-work. The most obvious example of directing energy occurs when casting the circle in the first place (see pages 130–131). In this case, you draw energy through your body and direct it through the solar plexus, down the arms and through the athame blade, wand or finger to form a circle of energy.

In a group there is sometimes a point when energy is released into the ether to go and do its work. An example of this can be found in healing work, where a circle of people holding hands first direct the energy they are about to raise to a named person or persons. They say the name aloud, then visualize that person well and happy. The group raises energy by moving deosil in a dance, perhaps chanting.There will be a point when everyone recognizes spontaneously that the energy has reached its optimum point. Some groups nominate a person to facilitate and judge when the energy is high enough and this person will signal when to release. Either way, when the time is ripe everyone raises their arms, hands still joined, and releases the energy skywards – sometimes with a shout or the last word of the chant to send it on its way. This does not break the circle, but it does release the energy raised for spell-work.

WICCA TOOLS

The two tools used most to direct energy in this way are the athame and the wand. The athame is used to cast circles, describe pentagrams and to direct energy when symbols are being 'named' as that which they represent. Wands can be used to cast circles, but are also deployed when the element of Air is invoked to carry the spell swiftly onwards.

Many witches use an athame or wand to direct energy raised for circle-casting.

POPULAR SPELLS

Humans don't come with feeding and care instructions attached, but we do come with a few basic needs. We need shelter, food, warmth, health, a purpose in life and love. The most commonly requested spells in the annals of magic roughly reflect this and within this chapter of the book you will find spells that represent these very human requirements.

LOVE AND VENGEANCE

The most popular spells are those to do with love and vengeance. In both cases, we carefully explain to the supplicants exactly why we can't give them what they want, and then offer them another way of looking at their situations. In the case of love, we cannot direct our magic towards a particular person, we cannot affect the free will of another, nor would we. If the supplicant is ready for love to come into their lives, then the spell on pages 154–155 is the answer. If, however, they are obsessed with a particular person because they feel that person's regard will validate them in some way, the problem is one of low self-esteem, and this may be better addressed using a healing spell (see pages 152–153).

All spells in this section are based on sympathetic magic – like representing through the use of symbols – the most common kind used in Wicca.

Before embarking on any of the spells, you are strongly advised to follow the advice given on page 88, which deals with one popular method of preparation for visualization, ritual and magical work.

USING THE SPELLS

The spells that follow are written as though a single person is performing them but they can easily be adapted for group-work. All spells should be performed inside a cast circle with the elements welcomed prior to beginning your work.

After all spell-work, close the sacral to third-eye chakras, leaving the base of spine and crown chakras very slightly open. Eat and drink in order to 'ground' yourself and return to your everyday state of consciousness. All candles should be allowed to burn down completely under supervision unless otherwise stated.

HEALING SPELL

Healing takes many forms and applies itself to many purposes, but be clear that healing magic is not about curing terminal diseases or performing miracles; remember we are working with the flow, not against it. If those suffering with terminal or chronic illnesses feel that they will benefit from having strength, calm and tranquility sent to them, then this is the healing that we can send. Sometimes spells do have remarkable results, but the truth is that we cannot change some things; but if we can offer other things that are needed, then we do.

TIMING

As this spell is for healing, you should work on a waxing or Full Moon. Sunday, ruled by the Sun, is the most auspicious day but always give priority to the Moon phase.

PREPARATION

Prior to casting this spell, try to identify exactly what is needed. Pinpoint it to its simplest expression so that you can concentrate on the core issue and focus the energy where it is needed most.

YOU WILL NEED

• Blue candle, 20 cm (8 in) in length

• Matches

• Fine paintbrush

• Small square plain paper

• Dot of red watercolour paint

• Small bowl of water

CASTING THE SPELL

1 Light the candle, saying: 'Welcome, element of Water, patron of healing and cleansing. Witness and empower the changes I weave in your name.'

2 Paint a red 'x' on the centre of the paper, saying: 'I name thee [name]'s pain/fear/anxiety.'

3 Hold the paper in front of you in both hands and focus on the red 'x'. Imagine the supplicant's problem encapsulated inside that one symbol.

4 Now place the paper in the bowl of water and move it around so that the paint disperses in the water and chant: 'I wash away this pain's offence. Be ye gone and get ye hence!'

5 Once the 'x' has become a pale smudge, remove the paper, crumple it up and throw it away.

6 To finish, pour the water into the Earth immediately after the circle, saying: 'So mote it be!'

Step 2

Step 4

LOVE SPELL

This spell is suitable for those who are ready for love to come to them. It signals that the supplicant is at a place in their lives where a loving relationship is desirable. It is most effective if the person asking for a new love carries out the spell for themselves. Otherwise, it is perfectly acceptable to cast this spell for someone else, provided that you are convinced that they are prepared to trust their wish to Spirit. Either way, it is necessary for the person asking for magical help to supply the crystals in this spell.

TIMING

Cast this spell on a waxing Moon, preferably on a Friday, ruled by lovely Venus.

PREPARATION

Leave the water for this spell out in the moonlight prior to casting the circle. In magic the Moon is a patron of the tides and this spell asks that a lover comes to the supplicant at the right time.

YOU WILL NEED

• Red candle, 20 cm (8 in) in length

• Matches

• Small tumbled rose quartz

• Small tumbled clear quartz

• Chalice or glass

• Water, 125 ml (4 fl oz)

• Red cloth, 25 cm (4 in) square

• Cord, 60 cm (24 in) in length

CASTING THE SPELL

1 Light the red candle saying: 'Passion burn bright like the Moon above me that I will meet with one who will love me.'

Step 1

2 Hold the rose quartz in one hand and the clear quartz in the other and visualize yourself walking on a sea-shore. A new love walks out of the waves towards you. As you walk towards each other, bring your hands together and transfer the clear stone to the hand holding the rose quartz.

3 Place the stones in the chalice and pour in the water, saying: 'May the light of the Moon bring the gift I desire. Washed in by the tide and blessed by the fire.'

Step 3

4 This 'fire' is the candle flame which should be allowed to burn down completely.

5 Leave the stones in the chalice for three days, before removing them and placing together in the red cloth which should be tied tightly into a pouch with the cord and worn about your neck for one Moon cycle.

Step 5

WEALTH AND WEAL SPELL

These days there is a tendency to see wealth as having more money than you could ever spend. However, 'wealth' in ancient societies carried a slightly different meaning and one that we would do well to learn from; it meant having sufficient for your needs. The term 'weal', from which 'wealth' is derived, referred to the yield of the land that accrued to the one that cultivated it. In a modern sense, 'Wealth and weal' imply material things that are needful and the capacity by which to ensure them. If you are considering casting this spell, do ensure that what you are asking for is needful.

TIMING

Cast on a waxing Moon for gain, and on a Thursday, ruled by generous Jupiter.

PREPARATION

Note especially in the case of spells for wealth that enchantments (for this is the method for this spell) tend to work best if you focus on the outcome only and leave the method to the wonders of the web of magic. Try to focus on the results you wish to achieve and do not speculate on how this will come about.

YOU WILL NEED

• Green candle, 20 cm (8 in) in length

• Matches

• Bread, pea-sized crumb

• Milk, 3 drops

• Sugar, 1 teaspoon

• Disused spider's web

• Saucer

• Red cloth, 25 cm (4 in) square

• Cord, 60 cm (24 in) in length

CASTING THE SPELL

1 Light the candle, saying: 'Goddess of the Earth, Goddess of the Hearth, I plant this spell to bring forth Wealth.'

2 Allow the bread to soak up the milk, then roll it in sugar and place inside the web.

3 Holding the bread and the web in your cupped hands, visualize the desired outcome while chanting: 'Silver of Moon, Gold of Sun, cast the spell and be it done.'

4 When you feel that you have thoroughly chanted your desire into the bread, sugar, milk and web, place them in the saucer.

5 Allow the candle to burn down completely in safety, then bury the mixture in Earth – preferably in your garden or window-box, as soon as possible the next day.

Step 1

Step 2

FERTILITY SPELL

As midwives and as layers-out of the dead, the Wise-woman or Cunning-man of a tribe or village were intimately connected with key physical rites of passage. Witches are still asked for charms and spells to promote reproductive fertility. Fertility takes many forms outside of pregnancy. This spell focuses specifically on helping a couple conceive – it must be emphasized that this applies to cases where there are no physical reasons why a couple are not conceiving – but it may be adjusted to focus on fertility in other areas, such as a blessing for crops, a garden or a project.

TIMING

The best Moon phases are the waxing or Full Moon for fertility and growth; and the best day is Monday as its patron, the Moon, rules matters of pregnancy and childbirth.

PREPARATION

Work this spell out of doors in a green field, preferably shortly after dawn; for safety's sake you may wish to take along a friend to watch and ensure you are undisturbed.

YOU WILL NEED

• Tea-light, white or green

• Needle

• Matches

• Clean jar

• Ripe corn, 9 ears

• Patchouli essential oil, 3 drops

• Green cloth, 10 cm (4 in) square

• Black cord, 60 cm (24 in) in length

CASTING THE SPELL

1 Using the needle, inscribe into the surface of the tea-light a downward-pointing triangle traversed halfway through by a horizontal line, while saying: 'Goddess of Earth, hold seeds of a birth.'

2 Now inscribe a waxing crescent moon, saying: 'Goddess of the Moon, swell the grain soon.' Light the candle and place it in the jar.

3 Facing the Sun, hold up the corn in your cupped hands, saying: 'Goddess of Fire, warm this desire.'

Step 1

4 Place the corn in the centre of the cloth and anoint with the patchouli oil. Bring the corners of cloth together and fasten into a pouch with the cord. Place the pouch in the centre of your circle and dance or walk around it nine times deosil; if you have mobility problems chant the three lines above three times each.

5 Give the pouch to the woman who desires the pregnancy to wear every night for the next three moons.

Step 4

PROTECTION SPELL

Sometimes we need to feel safe and shielded from the ill-will, envy or hatred of other people. Because part of 'opening up' to the Craft makes us sensitive to the atmosphere or energy that this can generate, it is good to renew our 'protection' on a regular basis. This is not to keep the world out – dealing with sometimes unpleasant situations and people is a part of life – but a protective shield can function to filter out the worst of the bad emotions that dysfunctional people may direct towards us. If we do not shield ourselves to some extent we would soak up the depression, pessimism and negativity and become unwell. This spell is a suitable antidote to that tendency.

TIMING

Cast this spell on a Dark Moon and on a Saturday, ruled by ringed Saturn.

PREPARATION

Prior to casting the circle, ensure that the charcoal is lit in the fireproof dish. Blend together the carrier oil and the cypress essential oil.

YOU WILL NEED

• Charcoal disc

• Fireproof dish

• Carrier oil, 1 teaspoon

• Cypress essential oil, 3 drops

• Black candle, 20 cm (8 in) in length

• Matches

• Dried juniper berries, 8

• Salt in single-holed dispenser

CASTING THE SPELL

1 Anoint the candle with the blended oil, rubbing first bottom to top, then top to bottom, then bottom towards top, stopping halfway up.

2 Light the candle, saying: 'Lilith of the Dark Moon, Hecate at the crossroads, Kali at the threshold.'

3 Place the berries on the red-hot charcoal. Pour a single ring of salt on to the floor around yourself, the candle and the incense, saying: 'I stand within protection of the Triple Goddess.'

4 Place your power hand (writing hand) on your heart and say: 'The protection of the Triple Goddess resides within me.'

5 Sit down inside the salt circle, concentrate on the candle-flame and visualize a shield of protection within and around you until you feel safe and confident. Blow away the salt circle with your breath and allow the candle to continue to burn down safely.

Step 1

Step 3

BANISHING SPELL

A banishing spell is not about making people disappear, although it might be tempting to fantasize that we could do this when someone is causing us distress. It is about dispelling bad behaviour and replacing it with a more appropriate quality. You need to give serious thought to the consequences before casting this spell. Whatever is banished must be replaced; magic abhors a vacuum; unless bad behaviour is replaced with something constructive, the person concerned will continue to be destructive.

TIMING

The best time for this spell is a waning Moon and the best day is Saturday, which is ruled by disciplinarian Saturn.

PREPARATION

If carrying out this spell on behalf of another, consider doing some healing work with that individual. Reassure them that in doing so you are not implying that the fault lies with them.

YOU WILL NEED

- Black candle, 20 cm (8 in) in length

- Matches

- Hair or signature of perpetrator

- Plain paper, 5 cm (2 in) square

- Pure alcohol, 1 teaspoon

- Epsom salts, 1 teaspoon

- Fireproof dish

- Heatproof mat

- Flower bulb, compost and pot

CASTING THE SPELL

1 Light the candle, saying: 'Old One, Wise One, Slow but sure One, Guide my spell and be it done.'

2 Hold up hair or signature, saying: 'I name thee [name]'s power.' Then wrap it in the paper and fold three times.

3 Place Epsom salts and alcohol in the fireproof dish (which you have placed on the heatproof mat) and light. Holding the folded paper say: 'As this Moon shrinks to bone, this spell shall burn your power down.' Throw the paper into the flame.

Step 3

4 Hold the bulb before the flame saying: 'Out of the ashes I name thee [quality you wish the subject to learn].' Plant the bulb in the compost, adding the ashes to the compost when cooled.

5 Give the plant to be tended to the one who requested your spell.

Step 4

RITUALS AND CEREMONIES

There is far more to ritual work than spells. Seasonal changes are celebrated at the eight Sabbats, the major festivals of the Wiccan year. The changing phases of the Moon are celebrated at Esbats, when we gather to honour the God and Goddess, to cast spells and to work on our own spiritual and magical development. The Sabbats and Esbats carry a personal element – as we celebrate seasonal and cyclical change in the world around us, we consider how these might be reflected in our own lives.

Wicca has evolved traditions to mark life changes.

Life-cycle rituals commemorate changes in our inner and outer worlds.

However, there are rituals that relate far more directly to the personal; rituals that help us to mark life events and celebrate rites of passage. Why perform a ritual? The significance of marking life-cycle or life-changing events with ritual in Wicca is that by enacting change symbolically within a sacred space, we send a message to our deepest spiritual selves, with the deities as witnesses. While in the circle we are working 'between the worlds', weaving new patterns that are 'registered' in the great web of existence. Because we are working symbolically, we are accessing our deeper consciousness. The effect of this dual impact brings about psychological and spiritual affirmation of the changes that have happened or are about to take place

It is possible to over-ritualize different aspects of our lives needlessly and this tendency is usually checked by the kindly counsel of a sister or brother practitioner early in our development in the Craft. It really isn't necessary to have a ritual for every single event, for example, before we leave the house or make a decision. In addition, rituals do not have to be elaborate, in fact, the simpler, the more effective, as a rule.

The following rituals are examples of ceremonies that you can perform for different key life-cycle events. They are designed to enable guests to be directly involved in the ceremony and can be adjusted accordingly. The basic structure assumes that you will be working with others within a cast circle, with officers for the elements who will light their respective candles when they have welcomed their element. All rituals in this section are very basic examples and can be easily recast to reflect your needs and preferences.

NAMING CEREMONY

This ritual is designed to enable friends and relatives to get involved at various stages of the ceremony, so agree beforehand who is to do what.

YOU WILL NEED

- An officer for each element

- Purification incense such as frankincense

- Chalice of water

- Loaf of bread

- Circlet of flowers for baby's head

- White candles in secure holders for each guest

PERFORMING THE RITUAL

1 Light the incense and cast a circle.

2 Officer for Air says: 'I welcome to this circle the element of Air with all its blessings. [To the baby] May you be blessed with learning and knowledge, with wit and the power to communicate easily with others.' Officer for Fire says: 'I welcome to this circle the element of Fire with all its blessings. May you be blessed with courage, the will and the strength to work for what is right.'

3 Officer for Water says: 'I welcome to this circle the element of Water with all its blessings. May you be blessed with love and friendship, and the gift of intuition.' Officer for Earth says: 'I welcome to this circle the element of Earth and all its blessings. May you be blessed with health, prosperity and knowledge of your roots in the Earth.' Officer for Spirit says: 'I welcome to this circle the element of Spirit and all its blessings. May you be blessed with wisdom and use your gifts to make the world a better place as you grow.'

4 The parent(s) then say: 'We are here to welcome a new baby to our family and our community, to ask that the Goddess watches over this little one and witnesses our wishes for her/him. [Speaking to the baby, placing the circlet on his/her head] We/I name you [name]. Welcome.' All those present say: 'Welcome [name].'

5 A chosen guest places a crumb of bread into the baby's hand, saying: 'May you never hunger and may you always have enough to share.' [To guests] 'May all present honour the trust that [baby] places in us as she/he grows.'

6 A second guest wets the baby's lips with water from the chalice, saying: 'May you never thirst and may you always have enough to share.' [To guests] 'May all present see this child raised with love.'

7 All guests step forward in turn to offer wishes for the little one, lighting a candle to seal it and placing it in the centre of the circle.

8 The parent(s) thank the guests, the element officers thank the elements and the circle is closed.

HANDFASTING

A pagan wedding is known as handfasting. This ceremony is traditionally for 'a year and a day', but here the commitment is for 'as long as love lasts', a common Wiccan vow. The ceremony outlined below is for different- or same-sex couples. You can incorporate readings or songs by friends and relatives. An exchange of rings is mentioned but you can forgo this and simply exchange promises. It is usual to use one's initiation cords to bind your hands, but new cord can be used and kept in a safe place afterwards.

YOU WILL NEED

- Love-incense lit prior to circle-casting

- Bread

- Chalice of wine or juice

- Cord

- Broomstick

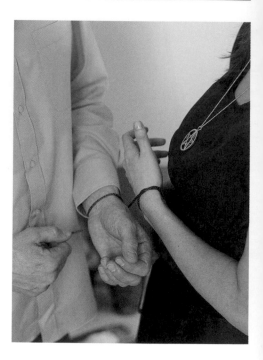

PERFORMING THE RITUAL

1 Cast a circle.

2 Officer for Air says: 'I welcome the element of Air which brings to this circle and this marriage the gifts of communication and good memories.' Officer for Fire says: 'I welcome the element of fire which brings to this circle and this marriage the gifts of loyalty and passion.' Officer for Water says: 'I welcome the element of Water which brings to this circle and this marriage the gift of love and patience.'

3 Officer for Earth says: 'I welcome the element of Earth which brings to this circle and this marriage the gifts of stability and a firm foundation.' Officer for Spirit says: 'I welcome the element of Spirit which brings to this circle and this marriage the gifts of wise choices in all that you do for and say to each other.'

4 Partner 1 says: 'Before this company, in this place and at this time I come to pledge my commitment to [name of Partner 2].' Partner 2 then says 'Before this company, in this place and at this time I come to pledge my commitment to [name of Partner 1].'

5 A chosen guest breaks a piece of bread in half and offers a piece to each partner, saying: 'May you never know want and always share what you have.' Another chosen guest offers each partner wine/juice from a chalice, saying: 'May you drink from the same cup and always remember the love you expressed for each other on this day/night.'

6 Partner 1 to 2 says: '[Name] I offer this ring, symbol of unity, with love and in trust and as a sign of my commitment to you.' Partner 2 repeats the same phrase.

7 Both partners wrap the cord around the wrists of their joined hands and, looking at each other, say in unison: 'I bind myself to you of my free will, I will honour your right to change and to grow, and I will support and love you in the best way I can, for as long as love lasts. So mote it be!'

8 Both partners jump over the broomstick. The handfasting is complete and the party can begin.

SEVERING CEREMONY

To handfast with another is to make a commitment within sacred space which resonates at a spiritual and emotional level. It is important, therefore, if a decision is made to separate, that you go into sacred space to sever that bond. Although endings can be painful, it is to be hoped that you can treat each other with the respect that you promised at your handfasting, and sort out your affairs in a civilized manner.

It is helpful to perform this ceremony together, whether alone or with witnesses. If this is not possible, the ritual can be adjusted to perform it alone. The outline that follows assumes that you are both present and have friends on hand to perform the offices required, including an Advocate to help you to get through the ceremony.

YOU WILL NEED

- Length of black cord long enough to go around both wrists, with about 30 cm (12 in) to spare

- Sharp athame

- Black candle

- Salt dispenser

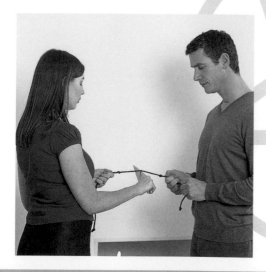

PERFORMING THE RITUAL

1 Cast the circle.

2 Officers welcome the elements as they normally would for an esbat. The Advocate says: 'We are here because [name 1] and [name 2] wish to part in honour and before the God and Goddess who blessed their joining together. [name 1] Do you agree that this is why you are here?' Name 1 responds: 'Yes.' The Advocate repeats the request to name 2 who should give assent.

3 Advocate lights the black candle at centre circle, saying: 'I invoke Saturn, Old One, Wise One, to witness the parting of [name 1] and [name 2]. May the Goddess who joined them now witness the severing of the bond and bless each of them as they journey their separate paths.'

4 The Advocate ties or asks the partners to tie the ends of the black cord around the wrist of the hand that was joined with that of their partner at the handfasting, leaving about 30 cm (12 inches) of cord stretched out between them.

5 Name 1 pours a line of salt on the floor between the partners, saying: 'Thus we are parted.' Name 2 takes the athame and severs the cord stretched between them, saying: 'Thus we are parted.'

6 The Advocate says: 'You have parted with honour; let the healing begin.' The black cord 'bracelets' should be removed after the ritual and buried deep in Earth far away from home.

SELF-BLESSING RITUAL

There are times after great change, after trauma or when we are suffering from self-doubt when we need spiritual sustenance. It is believed that this blessing ritual is based on a very ancient tradition; the salt represents the security and sanctuary of Earth and the candle flame represents moving from the fog of fear into the light of the Goddess's protection. The ritual below is designed specifically for solo work. The Dark Moon is the best time for self-blessing. However, as this ritual is only ever worked in times of need, it is likely that this, rather than the Moon phase, will be your priority. You should perform this ritual sky-clad – naked.

YOU WILL NEED

- White candle

- Salt

- A little pure olive oil

PERFORMING THE RITUAL

1 Cast a circle.

2 Welcome in the element of Air, saying: 'In the east the element of Air, I call you into the circle. Mighty Ones protect me.' Repeat this, moving deosil around the circle, calling in Fire, Water, and Earth in turn.

3 At the centre, welcome Spirit, saying: 'In the centre, at the margins and in all the spaces in between, element of Spirit guide and protect me.' Sprinkle the salt on the floor in front of you and step onto it saying: 'Earth beneath my feet offer me sanctuary from the cares of the world.' Light the white candle and step back from it.

Take the oil and anoint your feet, knees, sex, breast, lips, saying at the appropriate time:

Blessed be my feet that they may walk the sacred path

Blessed be my knees that they may never kneel in fear

Blessed be my womb/phallus without which we would not be

Blessed be my breast and the strong heart within

Blessed be my lips that they may speak Her will

4 Step into the light of the candle, saying:

I step into the light of the Goddess, into Her arms and into Her protection

Her light is my shield and Her embrace my armour

She walks with me in my footsteps

She is above and below me

To the East and the West of me

Before and behind me

Within and around me

5 Close your eyes and remain in the warmth and light of the candle for as long as your need directs you.

INDEX

ACKNOWLEDGEMENTS

Special Photography: © Octopus Publishing Group Limited/Russell Sadur

Other Photography: Alamy/Nigel Hicks 60–61. Bridgeman Art Library/Brian Shuel 58. Corbis UK Ltd/50, 124; /Jim Craigmyle 105; /Freelance Consulting Services Pty Ltd 120; /Greenhalf Photography 55; /Jason Hawkes 102; /David Muench 117; /Ted Spiegel 165; /Adam Woolfitt 118–19. Getty Images 166; /Adastra 137; /Robert Everts 15; /Fischer 56; /Planet Earth/Mike Coltman 96; /Jurgen Reisch 40; /Miquel S. Salmeron 17; /Adrian Weinbrecht 89; /Frank Whitney 59. Octopus Publishing Group Limited 14, 22, 32, 33, 53, 62, 71, 75, 125, 127 right; /Colin Bowling 37, 38; /Nick Carman 64; /Jerry Harpur 46; / Mike Hemsley 74,132, 133; /Sean Myers 41; Ian Parsons 57, 76 right, 127 left; /Guy Ryecart 81; /Roger Stowell 35; /Mark Winwood 122; / George Wright 54. Nasa 136. Rubberball 69.

With thanks to Mystics & Magic (www.mysticsandmagic.co.uk) for props borrowed on shoot.